Culture & Movement

Growing to know, love, & follow Jesus together by His grace

By Vince Bissey

© Vince Bissey

All rights reserved. No part of this publication may be reproduced, distributed, or transmitted in any form or by any means, including photocopying, recording, or other electronic or mechanical methods, without the prior written permission of the publisher, except in the case of brief quotations and certain other noncommercial uses permitted by copyright law. For permission requests, write to the publisher at the address below:

Vince Bissey
4642 Camellia Pl
Alton, IL 62002

"Most of our complaints are owing to unbelief, and the remainder of a legal spirit; and these evils are not removed in a day. Wait on the Lord, and he will enable you to see more and more of the power and grace of our High Priest. The more you know him–the better you will trust him. The more you trust him–the better you will love him. The more you love him–the better you will serve him. This is God's way. You are not called to buy–but to beg; not to be strong in yourself–but in the grace that is in Christ Jesus. He is teaching you these things, and I trust he will teach you to the end."

John Newton (March 18, 1767)

TABLE OF CONTENTS

Introduction | Powerful Simplicity

Chapter 1 | Intentionally Gospel-Centered Relationships

Chapter 2 | Living The Gospel Cycle

Chapter 3 | Inside-Out Christianity

Chapter 4 | What Matters To Jesus

Chapter 5 | Pro-Gospel

Chapter 6 | Pre-Gospel

Chapter 7 | Anti-Gospel

Appendix 1 | The Gift Of Repentance

Appendix 2 | The Gospel

Introduction

Powerful Simplicity

Growing up in the church made it far too easy for me to get comfortable with two lies:

1. "I know what the gospel is."
2. "I've moved beyond it."

While I wouldn't have said it out loud, I functionally believed that having agreed to Biblical doctrine and being determined to become the best version of myself, I had entered (at quite a young age, I might add...I was very precocious) the "coasting phase" of my life. All that was left was for me to kick back and wait for others to notice and congratulate me. I genuinely thought people would write books about me one day. Of course, I also thought that once I got married, I was going to have so much sex that I would lose weight. (Neither of these hypotheses has proven true...yet.)

But as Albert Einstein is rumored to have observed, "If you can't explain it simply, you don't understand it well enough." It wasn't until I became a dad, however, that I was truly put to the test. As a Christian father, one of my top priorities is to raise my kids "in the discipline and instruction of the Lord." (Ephesians 6:4) However, it didn't take long to realize that when talking to a two-year-old, no one was going to fill in the gaps of what I didn't understand except me. In that setting, I could no longer rely on common idiom, catchphrases, and the kindness of others wanting to assume the best about me. So in those conversations, it became painfully clear that my understanding of the gospel was vague and general at best.

The problem is that if you only understand the gospel in vague, general terms, then you'll only be able to live it out in vague, general ways. When this happens, it causes us to pull away from community (where we can be exposed) and to avoid Scripture (where we will be challenged), choosing instead to attend churches that are light on both. We do this so that we can keep up the front of maturity when, if we're honest, our greatest fear is being found out as gospel-frauds.

But what if our understanding of the gospel was clear and specific instead of vague and general? Imagine what it would feel like to always know your next step. Imagine always knowing how to pursue Jesus right in the middle of your struggles, no matter how deep your suffering or how dark your sin may be. As I was challenged to explain the gospel to my son, I began to understand that it is the God of the gospel who has the power, not the complexity of my explanation. Only Jesus has the power to save, and whatever we can do to embrace Him as our only hope will lead us deeper into the grace He purchased for us by His blood.

What is the Gospel?

So what is the gospel? Simply put, the gospel is: God-Sin-Grace-Glory. These four words capture the essence of the gospel, describing the overarching story of the Bible.

1. *GOD | God created all things.* The gospel is nothing if it's not God-centered, so a right view of God is necessary. That said, we have to realize that God is fundamentally holy but also fundamentally loving. God is holy and God is love, and His justice holds these glorious realities together in a perfect tension that we can't fully grasp.

2. *SIN | Mankind rebelled and continues to do so to this day.* The reason there's a tension at all, though, is because we have spit in the face of this holy God and we deserve nothing from Him but His deepest and fiercest wrath and punishment. Only when we begin with God's holiness can we rightly understand our sin, because it's only then that we see it in its true nature. Our sin is infinitely deserving of punishment because we have sinned against

an infinitely holy God. And yet God is love, and thus the tension. If God is to be holy and loving and just…there's got to be more to the story.

3. *GRACE | God responded to our rebellion by pursuing mankind in grace (from the promise in Genesis 3:15 forward to its fulfillment in Christ's death and resurrection).* In Jesus, we see the fullest picture of the grace of God restoring us to relationship with Him while at the same time perfectly fulfilling all three core aspects of His character. Paul says that on the cross, "God made Him who knew no sin to be sin for us, so that in Him we might become the righteousness of God." (2 Corinthians 5:21)

In other words, He took our badness and gave us His goodness. This is the great exchange. This is substitutionary atonement, and without it we have no gospel. God had identified Himself with His people and "in His divine forbearance He had passed over former sins," so that at the proper time He might show His righteousness, and so be both "just and the justifier of the one who has faith in Jesus." (Rom. 3:25-26) This faith is what unites us to Jesus in His life, death, resurrection, and glory, and this faith is a gift from God. It is God's to give to whomever He pleases, and the reason He does so for any of us is for His own glory.

4. *GLORY | God has done all this for His own glory (that is, He does all things not to show how great we are, but how great He is).* The true purpose of all things is the glory of God. We are called to delight in and seek after the glory of God in all things because that's what God does, and He invites us to join Him in it. God is building a universal and eternal empire–His kingdom–and He calls us to join Him in spreading a passion for His glory and a delight in all that He is for us in Jesus. This is what our mission is about. This is what discipleship is about. This is what the church is about. This is what life is about. It's not enough to merely say that God loved us so much that He was willing to send His Son to die for us. We must never leave out that He has loved for the sake of His

own glory. We could never deserve God's love. We could never earn God's grace. And we could never be a high enough prize for God to pay so great a cost–that is, unless He had a purpose higher than us. And this He does, namely His glory.

Who needs the Gospel?
God-Sin-Grace-Glory is the big story of the Bible, but it also explains the particulars of how God relates to each one of us. Yes, the gospel is God's story, but it's a story He invites us into. As we look for our place in God's story, we all come face to face with these simple facts:

1. My story starts with God because He formed me in my mother's womb and I am fearfully and wonderfully made in His image (see Psalm 139:13-16; Genesis 1:26-27);

2. I have rebelled against my creator and I have become His enemy by nature and by choice (see Romans 3:10-18). My sin is a debt I cannot pay, a weight I cannot carry, a stain I cannot clean, and a darkness I cannot escape.

3. Because this is true, my only hope for life, joy, and peace with God is if He does for me what I cannot do for myself. This means that when Jesus declared from the cross that "it is finished," (John 19:30) He was talking about the work He was doing to pay for my sin and make me a child of God.

4. As my Good Shepherd (John 10:11), Jesus now "leads me in paths of righteousness for His name's sake." (Psalm 23:3) Everything God does is for His glory and He invites me to join Him in His primary purpose for all things.

For those who have believed, the beginning and the end of our story is secure. We know God made us. We know that He's working "all things for the good of those who love Him" (Romans 8:28) and that "the earth will be filled with the knowledge of the glory of the LORD as the waters cover the sea." (Habakkuk 2:14) The problem comes when we're confronted with the fact that we're still living in the middle of the story: as sinners in need of grace.

Who is this book for?

And that's who this book is for: it's for those in the middle; it's for people in process; it's for sinners in need of the grace that only a sovereign, suffering, sacrificing Savior can provide. This book is for those who have been content with a vague, general gospel for too long and desire something more. This book is for people who need the power of a clear, specific gospel and know that this power can only come through a deepening relationship with Jesus Himself.

So as we begin, I want to challenge you to consider whether you've been led to believe the same lies I believed for so long:

1. Do you know the gospel?
2. Have you moved beyond it?

Once you can truly say "Yes" to the first question, you'll never again be able to say "Yes" to the second.

DISCUSS

1. How have you wrongly believed either that you know what the gospel is or that you have moved beyond it? How has that impacted your relationship with Jesus or with other people?

2. Have you ever felt like a "gospel fraud"? Why? How did you try to cope/compensate?

3. Re-read the section: "What is the Gospel?" How can this summary help you apply the gospel when it's most difficult?

4. How do you see the sin/grace dynamic play out in your day to day experience? How is it comforting that *"the beginning and ending of your story is secure"* (pg. 12)?

Chapter 1

Intentionally Gospel-Centered Relationships

Every local church has two distinct characteristics: Culture and Movement. Culture is simply how we answer the question: "*What are we inviting people into?*" Movement is how we answer the question: "*What are we inspiring people toward?*" These can be intentional or unintentional, positive or negative, but they're always both present.

Some churches invite you to belong or be a part of the family, but they inspire you to nothing beyond that. Some churches inspire you to achieve great things for God and His kingdom, while inviting you into little more than a club. And some invite you into dysfunction and inspire you to give up on the church altogether. But these are not the only options available to us as the people of God.

If we desire to create a Culture and a Movement that will be both positive and lasting, then we have to be intentional. For this to happen, however, every member of the church must seek to become both a catalyst for Culture and a conduit for Movement.

Catalysts for Culture

Culture is context. That is, "what we invite people into" is what gives shape to everything else we do as a community. This is why we've got to be intentional both to define and defend what is Biblically healthy so that we know what we're aiming at and what we need to guard against.

Defining Culture

While it's possible to express this in many different forms, any Biblical definition of Culture must include three essential elements: intentionally gospel-centered relationships.

First, a Biblically healthy Culture requires relationship. We bear the image of our Creator and we bear the name of our Redeemer, both of which point us to the centrality of community. Even before sin entered the picture, God declared: "It is not good that the man should be alone; I will make him a helper fit for him." (Genesis 2:18) We were created to need relationships. Not only that, we were also redeemed for relationship. By restoring us to right relationship with God through His life, death, and resurrection, Jesus now calls us to grow together as His body. As Paul put it: "Speaking the truth in love, we are to grow up in every way into Him who is the head, into Christ, from whom the whole body, joined and held together by every joint with which it is equipped, when each part is working properly, makes the body grow so that it builds itself up in love." (Colossians 4:15-16)

Second, a Biblically healthy Culture must be gospel-centered. Having relationships is necessary, but it isn't enough. For Biblical discipleship to be happening, our relationships must be gospel-centered.

What that means is:
- We must be focused on God rather than ourselves;
- We must be honest about our sin and the sin of others;
- We must give and receive the grace that Jesus died to purchase for us; &
- We must pursue the glory of God together more than any other shared passion, no matter how important it is.

When these things are truly happening, we will experience progress and growth both as individuals and as the body of Jesus: the church.

Third, a Biblically healthy Culture must be intentional. Gospel-centered relationships will not and cannot happen by accident. As followers of Jesus, we must be intentional to pursue not only Jesus, but also His people. We must resist the lies that we're too busy, that it's not that important, that we have nothing to offer, that we don't need other people, or that other people don't need us. In reality, we fight hardest for what we value most, and by God's grace, we are praying that Jesus will create a Culture of Pursuit among us by compelling us more and more to pursue intentionally gospel-centered relationships with God and one another.

Defending Culture

If any of these three elements of a Biblically healthy Culture is missing, we put ourselves and others in spiritual danger. It's like soul-pollution and the effects are often unidentifiable until permanent, deadly damage is done in our lives or the lives of those we love.

Because of this, it's important for us to defend a Culture of intentionally gospel-centered relationships. If we fail at this point, we open ourselves to *anonymity*, *affinity*, and *apathy*, all of which undermine the work of the gospel in the lives of God's people.

- <u>Intentionality + Gospel - Relationships = ANONYMITY</u>
Self-Promotion and Self-Protection are powerful motivators. Because this is true, it is the temptation of every human heart to hide from others, whether out of fear or out of pride. When this happens, we choose anonymity and cut ourselves off both from benefiting from the community and being a blessing to the community.

- <u>Intentionality + Relationships - Gospel = AFFINITY</u>
Too often, we use the church as a society to get connected with others who share our interests, hobbies, life-stage or goals. This can feel like Biblical community because the church organized our meeting, but where the gospel is absent, "the church" is nothing more than an incorrect name placed on a society/club.

- <u>Gospel + Relationships - Intentionality = APATHY</u>
Whether it's because we've convinced ourselves we don't really need people, or that they don't really need us, it is common even for the most Biblically informed Christians to be apathetic

about pursuing others. When this happens, it undermines their participation in the "one another" call of Scripture and inhibits the church from attaining its full potential as the body of Christ.

We can only defend against these enemies of Culture if we are aware of their existence, convinced of the dangers they pose, and committed to constantly evaluating ourselves and our community in light of what God calls the church to do and to be.

Developing Culture

How do we guard against these dangers? By developing a culture of intentionally gospel-centered relationships at three levels:

1. Our relationship with Christ;
2. Our relationships with the Church; &
3. Our relationships with the City.

How we cultivate these relationships will be the topic of later chapters. What we need to see here is that our relationship with Christ is at the core of every other relationship in our lives. Unless we're walking in deep, consistent, intimate communion with

Christ, our relationships with the church and with the city around us will remain shallow as well. In the same way, if we neglect deep, honest, grace-filled relationships with one another in the church, then our engagement in our city will be not only disingenuous, but even dishonest as we offer them something that we are not experiencing ourselves.

Conduits for Movement

Once God graciously does this work in us (Culture), only then should we expect God to work through us. And when He does, that is what we call Movement. If Culture is context, then Movement is momentum. It is the natural response of the human soul to the strength and beauty of the Divine. As we behold God in His majesty, we are moved to worship.

As we see the perfection of God's love in the cross of Jesus, we are moved to lay down our lives for one another. And as our eyes are opened to see "the light of the knowledge of the glory of God in the face of Jesus Christ," (2 Corinthians 4:6) we are moved to mission because we're convinced of the truth of the gospel and convicted by the Holy Spirit that we are not only recipients of grace but ministers of reconciliation. Because of this, we cannot help but be inspired to follow Jesus through suffering to glory, trusting Him to use us to accomplish the purposes for which He came: to save sinners (1 Timothy 1:15), build His church (Matthew 16:18), and manifest the name of the Father to a watching world which is desperate for grace (John 17:6, 26).

Movement is "what we inspire people to," and all Biblical movement begins with these four commitments:

1. *A Commitment to Pray | Asking & Expecting Jesus To Use Us.* Far too often, we give up on something before we really even try to succeed because we know that, in our own abilities and based on past experiences, we simply don't have the resources in ourselves to do what is expected of us. However, when Jesus promised that His Spirit would dwell in all who trust in Him, He was giving us the sure hope that in the power of the Holy Spirit, we are able to do all that Jesus commands and calls us to.

Therefore, when we see our insufficiency, it should drive us not to give up but to pray. When we hear the high calling to love one another, honor one another, serve one another, forgive one another, submit to one another, bear with one another, and encourage one another, we must honestly confess our weakness and sin that makes this feel impossible and we must pray for Jesus to do this in us by His Spirit, knowing that His grace is sufficient for us because His power is made perfect in our weakness (2 Corinthians 12:9).

2. *A Commitment to Pursue | Joining Jesus In Loving Sinners.* When Jesus said that He came to seek and save the lost (Luke 19:10), He was telling us in no uncertain terms that He is a pursuer. He pursued us in love even when we were His enemies and He continues to pursue us in love as His bride. Now Jesus invites all who have experienced His grace and been transformed by that love to join Him in this pursuit.

As John said it: "We love because He first loved us." (1 John 4:19) Therefore, when we experience the love of God, it should drive us not to withdraw but to engage. With Paul, we long to be able to say that "the love of Christ controls us" (2 Corinthians 5:14) as we live for Him who died for us. And as we lay down our lives in pursuit of others, our prayer is that *through our pursuit*, they might experience the pursuit of God Himself.

In other words, the calling to pursue intentionally gospel-centered relationships is a calling to follow Jesus in sacrificial love, and we can only do this by denying ourselves, taking up our cross, and following Him by grace.

3. *A Commitment to Preach* | *Proclaiming The Gospel With Gentleness & Respect*. When Peter told the church to always be ready to share the "reason for the hope that is in you," it was so that we would "honor Christ the Lord as holy" (1 Peter 3:15) not only with our lives, but with our words.

The gospel of Jesus is the good news of God's grace for sinners and, as such, it is the greatest need of every human heart. As we pray for and pursue others, we love and serve them only to the degree that we are willing, ready, and able to tell them the good news of Jesus and invite them to experience the hope of the gospel.

Therefore, when we hear others opposing the gospel of Jesus, it should drive us not to be silent but to preach. And when we do, we must preach *to people*, not *at people*. Peter describes this as "gentleness and respect," which flow from a heart that's convinced that we're sinners in need of grace as much as anyone else. We stand in solidarity with all who oppose us, so we're free to humbly, gently challenge and respectfully disagree as we show and tell others the love of Jesus.

4. *A Commitment to Practice* | *Doing What We Sing & Say*. For the church of Jesus to accomplish His vision of being disciples who make disciples, it's essential for us to be sincere at

every level. That is, it's not enough for us to gather to remember and rehearse the gospel; we must also go to adorn and obey this same gospel, surrendering all that we have and all that we are to the reign of King Jesus. And when we do, we tell the truth about Jesus not just with our lips but with our lives.

Therefore, when we hear the promise of Jesus that He will build His church (Matthew 16:18), it should drive us to action. When we hear the promise that "the earth will be filled with the knowledge of the glory of the LORD as the waters cover the sea" (Hab. 2:14), it should cause us to rejoice that we get to be a part of this plan of God as He works in and through the church of Jesus Christ to build His universal and eternal empire. And Jesus does it all through the powerful, transforming call: "Follow me." (Matthew 4:19, 8:22, 9:9, 10:38, 16:24, 19:21)

What happens when these work together?

The genius of the Great Commission is that Jesus didn't expect the first apostles to fulfill it on their own. No, in the same way that Paul would later point out that Jesus gave pastors to His church to "equip the saints for the work of the ministry," (Ephesians 4:11) the same dynamic is at play in Jesus' call to be disciples who make disciples.

Jesus knew that if we are true disciples, then we will make disciples. He also knew that if we make true disciples, then we are making disciple-makers. In this way, the church grows by multiplication, not merely addition, as the Holy Spirit works through the preaching of the gospel to raise up an army of missionaries who will "go into all the world," fully surrendered to Jesus' authority and fully secure in His presence (see Matthew 28:18-20).

Ultimately, this must be our aim if we want to be a Biblical church. Our longing is to see every image-bearing enemy of God become His child by grace through faith in the finished work of Jesus, and to see every child of God grow to full maturity in the life-giving, transforming work of the Holy Spirit. If we want to be a part of making this vision become reality, it will require two things of each one of us:

1. <u>We must BE disciples.</u> That is, each person must become a catalyst for a Culture of intentionally gospel-centered relationships; &

2. <u>We must MAKE disciples.</u> That is, each person must become a conduit for a Movement of God's people committed to praying for, pursuing, preaching to, and practicing their faith before a world in desperate need of grace.

That being said, it's important to recognize that these things can only happen if we can answer both: "*What does a disciple of Jesus actually look like?*" and "*How can we help move others to being and making these kind of disciples?*" The rest of this book is dedicated to answering those questions in a Biblical, practical way.

DISCUSS

1. How would you describe the "Culture" and "Movement" of previous churches you've been a part of?

2. In the description of a "gospel-centered relationship" (pg. 18), which of these is most difficult for you? Why?

3. If it's true that "we fight hardest for what we value most" (pg. 19), then how much do you value intentionally gospel-centered relationships?

4. Which of the 3 alternatives to intentionally gospel-centered relationships (Anonymity, Affinity, or Apathy) are you most tempted to settle for? Why?

5. Which of the 4 commitments on pg. 23-27 is most evident in your life right now? Which one needs attention?

6. How are you a Catalyst for Culture?
   How are you a Conduit for Movement?
   How *could* you be?

Chapter 2

Living The Gospel Cycle

So what does a disciple of Jesus actually look like? Similar to the need for simplicity and clarity when talking about the gospel, we need to pursue these same things when talking about Jesus' call to be disciples who make disciples. Perhaps more than any other reason, this is due to the fact that "disciple" has become a buzzword in a Christian subculture. That is, it has become popular through broad use, but it lacks clarity for the exact same reason. The problem is: <u>we can't pursue what we</u>

can't define. Whether you're running a business, coaching a football team, raising a family, or planning a vacation, it's impossible to make any progress until a goal is clearly identified. Only then can you begin to form a strategy by which to accomplish it. To be sure, without a clear goal you can still collect a paycheck, play a game, procreate, and travel. But without a well-defined "win," we can never know if we're moving in the right direction or when we've achieved success.

How The Bible Speaks About Discipleship
As God's breathed-out word (2 Timothy 3:16), the Bible must be our starting point for clarity and understanding of what a disciple is and does. As we begin exploring what the Bible says about discipleship, however, it is important to note that this is a rare concept in the Old Testament. In Isaiah 8:16, the prophet gives instructions for the words of Yahweh to be bound up and sealed "among my disciples." In this context, as well as in the other 5 uses of the word in Isaiah and Jeremiah, "disciple" means "taught ones," which is exactly how the concept is used when we come to the New Testament.

As the New Testament opens, we quickly discover a very different emphasis. No doubt taking their cue from Jesus (since it was clearly not a major theme in the Old Testament), the Gospel writers used the Greek word for "disciple" 238 times. Whether describing the general student-teacher relationship (Matthew 10:24-25), one devoted to a specific teacher like Moses (John 9:28) or John the Baptist (Luke 7:18-19), or one devoted to a specific school of teaching like the Pharisees (Mark 2:18), the basic sense of "disciple" is always that of a "learner."

When this word is used for disciples of Jesus, however, we need to realize that Jesus was never content with just passing on knowledge. No, for His disciples, Jesus' goal was to teach them in order to train them. It wasn't enough for them to understand and agree with what He taught them, they needed to trust what He promised them and follow where He led them. We see this clearly in John 8:31, where Jesus told the believing Jews that "if you abide in my words, you are truly my disciples." Likewise, in John 15:8 He said, "By this my Father is glorified, that you bear much fruit and so prove to be my disciples."

For Jesus, a disciple was a learner not of a school of thought, but of a way of life.

This understanding of "disciple" was solidified by the time Luke wrote the book of Acts. In fact, all 28 occurrences of the term are synonymous with how we use the word "Christian" today (see Acts 11:26 for the origin of this shift). Is it possible for someone to claim to be a Christian and yet lack genuine faith? Is it possible to mistake someone's external actions for internal heart-change? Is it possible to intentionally deceive others into thinking one is a Christian for the sake of personal gain or reputation? Of course.

But just as we would identify such a person as an impostor, a deceiver, or even just confused, we would never define what a Christian is or should be by these false claims. In the same way, what we see in Acts is that discipleship is always defined by devotion. So much so, in fact, that the growth of the church and expansion of the kingdom of Jesus is measured at key points throughout the book by the growing number of disciples (see especially Acts 6:1-7).

Perhaps what is most intriguing, however, is that when we turn from Acts to Romans and read the rest of the New Testament, the word "disciple" is never used again. Not by Paul, not by Peter, not in Hebrews, not by Jude or James (the brothers of Jesus), and not by John (the "disciple Jesus loved"). But if this was such an important concept for Jesus and the Gospel writers, why is it completely absent in the New Testament letters?

How The Bible Shows Discipleship

The simple answer to this question is that these authors didn't continue using the word "disciple" because their goal wasn't verbal consistency, but conceptual consistency. That is, they were intent on adapting the teaching and truth of Jesus to the varying cultures where He sent them to proclaim it (see Acts 1:8). As a result, what was important wasn't their use of a specific word, but their embodiment of a reality, and this is exactly what we see throughout the New Testament letters.

The question we need to ask, then, is not "Where is the word 'disciple' used?" but rather "What does a disciple of Jesus look like in the New Testament?"

And as usual, when we ask the right question, the answer is right there on the surface just waiting for us to see it.

There are three essential threads that are woven throughout the entirety of the Bible from Genesis to Revelation:

- The importance of knowing God as He has revealed Himself to us;
- The importance of loving God for who He is and what He's done for us; &
- The importance of following God's law, surrendering to His will, and obeying His commands.

With the incarnation of Jesus, the life and teachings of Jesus, the cross and resurrection of Jesus, the preaching of the gospel of Jesus, and the promise of the return of Jesus, we see in the New Testament that all who want to be faithful to the God of the Bible will seek Him in and through Jesus, His Son. This is first demonstrated by Simeon (Luke 2:25) and Anna (Luke 2:36-38), who were just two examples of how an entire generation of faithful, God-fearing Jews were waiting for the arrival of their Messiah.

Jesus Himself affirms this over and over, saying things like "If you believed Moses, you would believe me, for he wrote of me" (John 5:46); and "Everything written about me in the Law of Moses and the Prophets and the Psalms must be fulfilled." (Luke 24:44)

It is on the foundation of this core truth that Jesus proceeds to build out what a true disciple (i.e. learner/follower) really looks like. It shouldn't surprise us, then, that it includes all the same elements that have always been included in faithfulness to God, only now they are focused on Jesus, who is "the radiance of the glory of God and the exact imprint of His nature." (Hebrews 1:3)

In Matthew 28:18-20, Jesus gave us the Great Commission, calling us to obey Him in every area of life based on a new identity in His person and work. Luke 9:23 tells us all discipleship begins with the call of Jesus to follow Him; something we can only do when we deny ourselves and take up our cross. In John 10:14-15, Jesus says "I am the good shepherd. I know my own, and my own know me."

A few chapters later in John 14:15, He says "If you love me, you will keep my commandments."

After His resurrection, the apostles of Jesus continued to emphasize and prioritize all these same characteristics. That is, they show us the same truth in different words. One of the clearest places we see this is in the prayers of Paul for the churches he wrote to.

In Philippians 1:9-11, Paul told the church: "It is my prayer that your love may abound more and more, with knowledge and all discernment, so that you may approve what is excellent, and so be pure and blameless for the day of Christ, filled with the fruit of righteousness that comes through Jesus Christ, to the glory and praise of God." Paul's prayer for the church includes the same three elements Jesus emphasized and the Old Testament insisted on: knowing, loving, and following Jesus. But it's important to notice here that Paul's prayer, above all, is for love.

So that's where Paul begins, praying that their "love will abound more and more."

With that as his goal, Paul also prays that this will happen "with knowledge and all discernment" because we can't love God deeply if we don't know God truly. And as the church grows in knowing and loving God, Paul prays that they will become more like Jesus ("pure and blameless") and that they would be filled with "the fruit of righteousness that comes through Jesus Christ." In other words, good works flow out of a heart that loves God. And in it all, Paul has one end in mind: "the glory and praise of God."

Gospel Cycle
To grow as disciples means we are growing to know, love, and follow Jesus more.

That is, we're living the Gospel Cycle:
- The more we know Jesus, the more we will love Him.
- The more we love Jesus, the more we will follow Him.
- The more we follow Jesus, the more we will know Him.
- [Repeat]

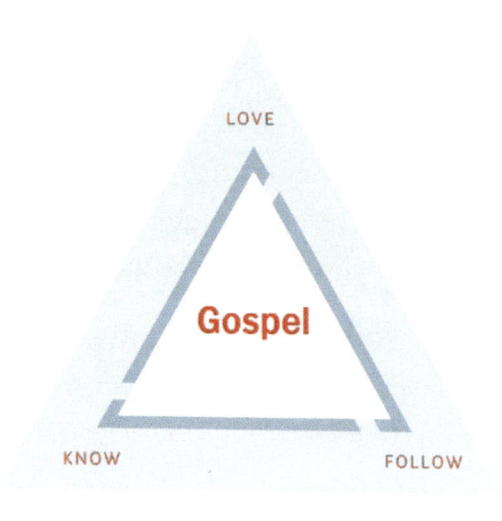

Defining Our Terms

With this as our goal, it's important for us to be clear about what we mean and don't mean by each of these statements. Only then will we be able to rightly evaluate where we are starting from and where we need to take our next steps toward growth, which is what we will consider in the next chapter.

KNOWING JESUS

What It Isn't

- *The Philosopher* | Knowing Jesus truly doesn't require us to be intellectuals. It is a common theme in Scripture that those with the greatest amount of factual knowledge about God and His Word (i.e. Demons and Pharisees) were the same ones receiving the sharpest condemnation from Jesus for not truly knowing Him.

- *The Politician* | Likewise, knowing Jesus is not the same as talking about Him positively whenever it is convenient or expected. To use Jesus' name or teachings for personal gain (whether it's to gain a vote or get a girlfriend) is a masquerade that shows one does not truly know Jesus as they ought.

What It Is

We believe that Jesus is the full revelation of the Father, and that God reveals Himself in Christ, through Scripture, by the Holy Spirit. As a result, we can know Him truly even though we cannot know Him fully. Likewise, we must embrace the full word of God and submit to all of it as God's self-revelation.

We don't sit over God's word but under it. We do not judge God's word, but it judges us.

Therefore, to know Jesus truly is to know Him on His terms, not our own. It means we respond to His revelation instead of making it up as we go along. As we choose God's self-revelation (in the Scriptures and in Jesus) over human reason, we trust His promise that this path of full surrender is the only path to lasting freedom and joy (see Psalm 19:7-14).

LOVING JESUS

What It Isn't

- *The Feeler* | Loving Jesus is not the same as emotionalism. Tears may accompany confession of sin and grief may accompany repentance, but to assume that tears and grief are the same as confession and repentance is an error that has kept many from experiencing the true, blood-bought grace of Jesus. Why? Because when we base our forgiveness on our feelings instead of His promises, the focus is turned once again to us, which is why we need to confess and repent in the first place.

- *The Showman* | Some will try to compensate for a lack of knowledge and/or genuine love for Christ by excessive outward expression. The problem is: when the external doesn't match the internal, this is the peak of hypocrisy. There is no doubt that deep movement of soul may well be the result of beholding the glory of God shining in the face of Jesus Christ and should lead us to our knees in reverent awe before our holy God. However, this is not the same as a mindless frenzy designed to draw attention not to the One being worshipped, but to the worshipper.

What It Is

To love Jesus as the Bible invites us to requires that our hearts be engaged, not just our minds. At the same time, this love must be rooted in and flow out of our knowledge of Jesus. Only then will it be the kind of love for Jesus which brings a re-centering of our entire lives on His character, His work, and His promises. And this kind of love is always a response from God's people because we understand that not only did God love us first (1 John 4:19) but also that what we love most determines what we live for. By God's design, we are all worshippers and the question is never *if* we will worship but *who*: the Creator or the Created (see Romans 1:21-25)? As we receive and rest in the love of Jesus, our hearts will respond in kind, loving the God who made us, pursued us, became one of us, lived among us, died for us, rose victorious from death and now reigns at the right hand of His Father until He returns to finish what He started and take us home to live with Him forever. This is our King and our Savior, and He alone is worthy of our worship, awe, fear, and praise, both now and for eternity.

FOLLOWING JESUS

What It Isn't

- *The Activist* | Following Jesus faithfully is not the same as being a fan of His teaching, agreeing with His politics, or appreciating His example. Everything from Biblical morality to the gospel itself can be twisted in the hands of the Activist into the service of a pet cause, thus making God's will and word the means to an end instead of the end itself.

- *The Legalist* | Similarly, following Jesus is often reduced to mean simply doing what He said. However, when the emphasis is on doing before being, external obedience becomes the sole focus and the faith Jesus consistently requires of us becomes irrelevant. For the Legalist, faith is viewed and treated as another work done to warrant/earn God's favor.

What It Is

As mentioned before, Jesus was clear that all who love Him will do what He commands (John 14:15). In other words, love for Jesus not only precedes, but also produces obedience to Him. What that means is that any external obedience that does not flow from a heart of love for Christ is, in fact, a form of moral rebellion against the cross of Jesus.

In Romans 1:5 and 16:26, Paul bookends the greatest proclamation of the gospel ever written with the simple fact that this gospel is what brings about the "obedience of faith." In the same letter, Paul is clear that "whatever does not proceed from faith is sin." (Romans 14:23).

When held up side by side, this shows that even the greatest acts of external obedience, if not done from a heart of faith in Jesus and love for Jesus, are nothing but white-washed sin, giving false hope to all who are content with an appearance of godliness while denying its power (see 2 Timothy 3:5).

From beginning to end, the Bible is clear that this is what it looks like to be a disciple of Jesus. What we need to remember, though, is that the Bible is just as clear that as we grow as disciples, we will also grow in our desire to make disciples, helping others experience that growth together with us as we grow to know, love, and follow Jesus together by His grace.

DISCUSS

1. How can/should we measure internal spiritual growth without reducing everything to external actions and missing the heart?

2. Where have you been a disciple ("learner") of a school of thought more than of Jesus Himself? What did that produce in you? How can you guard against that?

3. Regarding the Gospel Cycle:
   –What do you find helpful?
   –What do you find confusing?

4. Read each pair of "What It Isn't" descriptions and consider:
   –Where have you seen this in yourself?
   –Where have you seen this in the church?

5. Read each "What It Is" description and consider:
   –How has God been doing this in your life?
   –What can do to pursue growth in this area?

Chapter 3

Inside-Out Christianity

The missional movement of the early 21st century has been disruptive to the traditional church in all the right ways. Based on Paul's observation that there's no such thing as a "seeker" (Romans 3:11), it has challenged the church to take the hope of the gospel to a dying world instead of expecting that world to come knocking on our doors. Based on the belief that Scripture is a missionary handbook which can be adapted for every generation and society, it has challenged the church to engage culture in their terms, but not on their terms. And based on the depths of God's grace revealed in the gospel, it has reminded the church that sin is the only precondition for receiving God's mercy, so it shouldn't surprise us or scare us when we see sin in ourselves or others, but rather it should drive us to the cross of Jesus. All of these things should humble us and, at the same time, lead to increased confidence in Christ because we are fully known and deeply loved.

All these things are gifts the missional movement has given to the church. However, as with any corrective action, no matter how much it may be needed, the risk is always to go too far in one direction or another. In the case of the missional movement, this risk is most evident in two tendencies:
1. Under-emphasizing holiness in the fight against legalism; &
2. Over-emphasizing mission in the fight for Biblical faithfulness.

Under-Emphasizing Holiness
In the fight against legalism, the risk which has become evident in the missional church has been the

tendency to neglect preaching the clear commands of Scripture. Whether this is rooted in the preacher's fear of being misunderstood or in the misunderstanding of the preacher himself, the result of such preaching is a distorted view of God. The Biblical portrayal is that He is a God of radical, strong, beautiful, majestic holiness and that for mere mortals to approach His presence means certain death apart from His gracious intervention because, like Isaiah, we are a community of the unclean and we cannot presume to look upon the King, the LORD of hosts, and live (see Isaiah 6:5). In addition to this, the Scriptures repeatedly return to God's command to His people: "Be holy for I, the LORD your God, am holy." (Leviticus 11:44-45; 19:2; 20:7, 26; 21:8; 1 Peter 1:15-16)

But this is not the full picture, because while the holiness of God shows us how far short we fall, it also reveals to us the perfection of Jesus Christ, who is "the radiance of the glory of God and the exact imprint of His nature," (Hebrews 1:3) but who can still sympathize with our weaknesses because He "in every respect was tempted as we are, yet without sin." (Hebrews 4:15)

In Ephesians, Paul adds that it was to make us holy that "God chose us in Christ before the foundation of the world" (Ephesians 1:4) and that "Christ loved the church and gave Himself up for her, that He might sanctify her, having cleansed her by the washing of water with the word, so that He might present the church to Himself in splendor, without spot or wrinkle or any such thing, that she might be holy and without blemish."
(Ephesians 5:25-27)

In light of these things, to fail to call men and women to holiness is to undermine God's character, minimize the depth of our rebellion, misrepresent the blessing of full surrender to the Lordship of Christ in obedience to His commands, lose the joy of repentance, and consign the church under our leadership to false contentment in what God clearly reveals that He hates because it pulls us away from Him.

To be sure, we must never fall into the legalistic lies that God judges us based on our works or that perfection in this life is possible. These are dangerous and false doctrines that put the focus on us and make us deserving (at least partially) of grace. However, while we're judged based on the work of Jesus (not our own) and we are never perfect in this life, we are always called to "strive for the holiness without which no one will see the Lord," (Hebrews 12:14) trusting that God gives to us all that He requires of us and that He does this in and through Jesus, our Redeemer.

Over-Emphasizing Mission

In light of the Great Commission and the call of the church to be disciples who make disciples, it may seem puzzling (or even wrong) to suggest that we can over-emphasize something so central and significant to what it means to be faithful to Christ. It's helpful to remember here, though, that to value the right things in the wrong order can lead to problems, even if you value all the right things. This shows up regularly in conversations with couples who have just gotten married. It is a common temptation for a young man to be so smitten with his new bride that he begins to value, pursue, and invest in his relationship with her with greater intensity and with greater attention than he's investing in his relationship with Jesus. This most often occurs without him even realizing it of course, but that doesn't prevent it from causing him to expect her to give him what he should be seeking from Christ alone (things like identity, calling, purpose, joy, contentment, etc...). In so doing, the young man puts more weight on the relationship than it was ever designed to bear and he begins to actually do damage to what he loves most precisely because his love isn't rightly ordered. The only healthy way for this young man to love his bride as he ought is if he loves Jesus most of all and leads her to do the same. When this happens, their love will have a solid foundation on which to build a life together till death separates them.

In the same way, in the fight for Biblical faithfulness to the Great Commission, the risk to the missional movement is like that of a young man with his new bride. The temptation is to so emphasize and focus on the mission that we neglect to prioritize, as of first importance, our pursuit of Jesus and His church. As we saw in Chapter 1, God has created us for and called us to pursue intentionally gospel-centered relationships within three spheres: Christ, Church, and City.

Christ

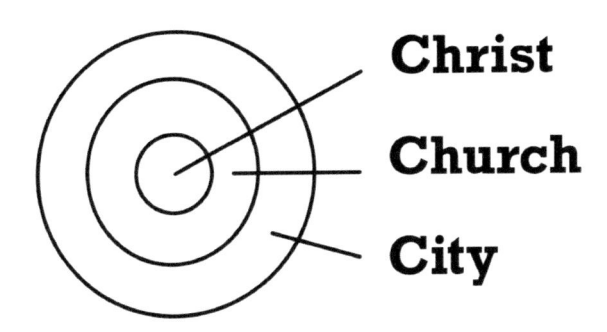

Church

City

If we neglect to cultivate our relationship with Christ as the core of who we are and the foundation we're building everything else upon, then our relationships within the church will never thrive according to God's design. This is because it is our shared union with Christ which unites us to one another. Jesus is the Head and each member of His body, by virtue of being connected to the Head, is likewise connected to every other member and called to function in harmony as one body (see Romans 12:4-5). Unless each member of the body is growing to know, love, and follow Jesus individually, we will never grow to do this together as He calls us to.

In the same way, if we neglect to cultivate oneness and genuine love for others in the church, then all the growth God may bring us as a result of faithful missional engagement in the city will be stunted due to the fact that we're inviting outsiders to join a dysfunctional body barely connected to its true Head.

Inside-Out Christianity

The antidote to both of these tendencies is an "inside-out" perspective on God, His world, and our place in it as His people. In the same way that we must learn what it means to be disciples before we can faithfully make disciples, so we must be growing personally before we'll be able to fully contribute to and participate in the growth of the church.

Up to this point, the goal has been to provide a simple understanding of what it means to be a disciple of Jesus. However, before we effectively consider how to make disciples, we need to reflect on and evaluate where we're starting from so that we can know what next steps are needed for us personally. To do this, the remainder of this chapter provides a process for you to identify where you are and where you need to grow.

This process includes four steps:
- Step 1 | Embracing the Mission
- Step 2 | Honest Self-Analysis
- Step 3 | Setting Personal Goals
- Step 4 | Taking Action Together

Step 1 | Embracing the Mission.
For us to devote our lives to growing to know, love, and follow Jesus together by His grace, we have to first be convinced that this is, in fact, the calling He has given us in His word. Take a moment to reflect on what we've discussed up to this point. Identify points of disagreement and/or misunderstanding and commit to discussing these with a pastor or trusted friend before taking the next step. Doing so will ensure alignment and help you fully embrace the process as God guides you through a time of prayerful self-analysis and goal-setting.

Step 2 | Honest Self-Analysis
With knowing, loving, and following Jesus as our grid, we need to begin with honest self-analysis before we can set realistic and helpful personal goals for growth.

For each of the statements below, give yourself a score from 1 (Completely False) to 5 (Completely True).

KNOWING JESUS

___ I have a plan for consistent, intentional Bible reading.

___ I regularly read books or listen to sermons during the week to help me understand and apply the gospel.

___ I am able to explain the gospel simply and fully in less than 2 minutes.

___ I seek out theological conversations with friends.

___ I am able to apply God's promises to specific struggles in life.

___ I regularly notice when a preacher, teacher, friend, or celebrity says something incorrect about what the Bible teaches.

___ I have a basic understanding of the historical context for any book of the Bible I read.

___ I know how and where to find answers to questions about God, the Bible, and the gospel.

___ I know and use study methods to help me better understand God's truth revealed in the Bible.

___ I am not satisfied with hearing about God from others, I want to learn directly from God Himself.

Add up your answers for this category and write your score:

___ / 50

LOVING JESUS

___ God consistently reminds me of His love for me.

___ I seek out people, stories, songs, and experiences that will stir up my affections for Jesus.

___ I have a plan for regular, intentional prayer and personal worship.

___ I regularly meditate on the gospel and how much I need God's grace.

___ A book, sermon, or song that is theologically correct but emotionally cold and dry is a contradiction.

___ My highest goal in life is experiencing more joy in Jesus.

___ I get excited to learn new things from the Bible because that's where Jesus reveals Himself most clearly.

___ I look forward to worshiping Jesus weekly by singing with the church.

___ My desire is to worship Jesus in every area of life.

___ I am not satisfied with learning about God, I want to experience His presence and power.

Add up your answers for this category and write your score:

___ / 50

FOLLOWING JESUS

___ I have people in my life who help me identify blind spots and challenge me to surrender all to Jesus.

___ I regularly evaluate my actions, thoughts, feeling, and motives in light of God's will revealed in the Bible.

___ There are no secret sins in my life that I'm continuing to knowingly embrace.

___ I see God's commands as invitations to grow.

___ Nothing in this life is worth disobeying God to have it.

___ Faith in Jesus should always produce faithfulness to Jesus.

___ I feel my own inability to obey Jesus but I'm depending on the Holy Spirit to work in and through me so that I can.

___ I see the Great Commandment (love God and love others) & the Great Commission (be disciples who make disciples) as exciting opportunities to be part of His work in the world.

___ Repentance is a regular rhythm in my life.

___ I am not satisfied with experiencing God's presence unless I am becoming more and more like Jesus.

Add up your answers for this category and write your score:

___ / 50

Step 3 | Setting Personal Goals
Just as we have to know where we are if we hope to make progress toward where we want to go, it's just as true that we have to know where we're going if we ever hope to get there. And that's where goal-setting comes in.

In light of your self-evaluation above, develop three S.M.A.R.T. Goals that will help you build on where you're strong and develop where you're weak as you grow to know, love, and follow Jesus more by His grace.

If this is unfamiliar to you, S.M.A.R.T. Goals are:

- Specific | You know exactly what you're aiming at;
- Measurable | You know how you are progressing;
- Attainable | You can actually achieve this goal;
- Relevant | You truly care about accomplishing this goal; &
- Timed | Your goal has a deadline.

Focus	S.M.A.R.T. Personal Goals
Know Jesus	
Love Jesus	
Follow Jesus	

Step 4 | Taking Action Together

One gift of the gospel is that we're never alone. In Christ, God is with us and for us. He has given us His Spirit to dwell within us and bear fruit for His glory. And He's given us the church to encourage us, pray for us, and build us up in love (Ephesians 4:16).

So after you set your personal goals, the next step is to invite at least one other person to pray for you, hold you accountable, and encourage you as you pursue these goals. Decide who that will be and follow up with them as soon as you're able in order to establish a rhythm of challenge and encouragement as you decide together how to most effectively pursue these goals for God's glory and your joy.

- For Goal #1 (Knowing Jesus):

  _____

- For Goal #2 (Loving Jesus):

  _____

- For Goal #3 (Following Jesus):

  _____

"May the God of endurance and encouragement grant you to live in such harmony with one another, in accord with Christ Jesus, that together you may with one voice glorify the God and Father of our Lord Jesus Christ." (Romans 15:5-6)

DISCUSS

1. Prior to reading this, what benefits and/or drawbacks would you have identified regarding the "Missional Movement" in the 21st Century Church?

2. Where have you been tempted to "neglect preaching the clear commands of Scripture" (pg. 51)? Why do you think this occurs?

3. If "Moralism" is caring more about the external actions than the internal motivations of an individual, "Missionalism" is caring more about the actions than the motivations of a church.
   –How do you see this in the church today?
   –How does the "inside-out church" address this?

4. For each set of "Honest Self-Analysis" questions, either evaluate each question together or discuss:
   –Which question was most encouraging?
   –Which question was most challenging?
   –How is God leading you to pursue change?
   –What does that look like from an "inside-out" perspective?

Chapter 4

What Matters to Jesus

As we've seen, the Bible is clear that if we want to be faithful disciples of Jesus, we will individually be pursuing growth in knowing, loving, and following Jesus. The Bible is just as clear, however, that while this is necessary for each of us, none of us can do it alone. As Paul says it in Romans 12:4-5, "As in one body we have many members, and the members do not all have the same function, so we, though many, are one body in Christ, and individually members one of another."

In other words, when Jesus makes us one with Him by grace through faith, He not only makes us one with the Father (as children of the living God - Romans 9:26), but He also makes us one with each other (as the church of the living God - 1 Timothy 3:15). Therefore, as individuals, we can't follow Jesus faithfully unless we love Him deeply and know Him truly. Likewise, none of us can claim that we are following Jesus faithfully unless we are pursuing Him together with His people. As a result, our mission must always be to grow to know, love, and follow Jesus together.

According to Jesus, if we desire to accomplish this mission, it's going to require the church to care about and prioritize the same things He did: worship, community, and mission. In John 17, we get the privilege of listening in on the final prayer of Jesus for His people before He went to the cross. He prays for Himself, for His disciples, and for all who would believe as a result of their faithful testimony to Him. And woven throughout the entire prayer, we see again and again how Jesus returns to these three themes because these are not only the reason He came, but the reason He was preparing to die.

Jesus sacrificed everything so that His people would be able to follow Him into worship, community, and mission. Before we draw attention to specific aspects of this prayer, though, the most helpful thing is to simply read it in its entirety and let Jesus speak for Himself:

John 17 (ESV)

Jesus Prays for Himself

"When Jesus had spoken these words, he lifted up his eyes to heaven, and said, 'Father, the hour has come; glorify your Son that the Son may glorify you, 2 since you have given him authority over all flesh, to give eternal life to all whom you have given him. 3 And this is eternal life, that they know you, the only true God, and Jesus Christ whom you have sent. 4 I glorified you on earth, having accomplished the work that you gave me to do. 5 And now, Father, glorify me in your own presence with the glory that I had with you before the world existed.

Jesus Prays for His Disciples

6 "I have manifested your name to the people whom you gave me out of the world. Yours they were, and

you gave them to me, and they have kept your word. [7] Now they know that everything that you have given me is from you. [8] For I have given them the words that you gave me, and they have received them and have come to know in truth that I came from you; and they have believed that you sent me.

[9] I am praying for them. I am not praying for the world but for those whom you have given me, for they are yours. [10] All mine are yours, and yours are mine, and I am glorified in them. [11] And I am no longer in the world, but they are in the world, and I am coming to you. Holy Father, keep them in your name, which you have given me, that they may be one, even as we are one. [12] While I was with them, I kept them in your name, which you have given me. I have guarded them, and not one of them has been lost except the son of destruction, that the Scripture might be fulfilled. [13] But now I am coming to you, and these things I speak in the world, that they may have my joy fulfilled in themselves. [14] I have given them your word, and the world has hated them because they are not of the world, just as I am not of the world. [15] I do not ask that you take them out of the world, but that you keep them from the evil one.

[16] They are not of the world, just as I am not of the world. [17] Sanctify them in the truth; your word is truth. [18] As you sent me into the world, so I have sent them into the world. [19] And for their sake I consecrate myself, that they also may be sanctified in truth.

Jesus Prays for His Church

[20] "I do not ask for these only, but also for those who will believe in me through their word, [21] that they may all be one, just as you, Father, are in me, and I in you, that they also may be in us, so that the world may believe that you have sent me. [22] The glory that you have given me I have given to them, that they may be one even as we are one, [23] I in them and you in me, that they may become perfectly one, so that the world may know that you sent me and loved them even as you loved me.

[24] Father, I desire that they also, whom you have given me, may be with me where I am, to see my glory that you have given me because you loved me before the foundation of the world. [25] O righteous Father, even though the world does not know you, I know you, and these know that you have sent me.

²⁶ I made known to them your name, and I will continue to make it known, that the love with which you have loved me may be in them, and I in them.'"

What Jesus Prayed For

One of the most obvious features of this prayer of Jesus is who He was praying for. I added headings to the text to make it explicit, but even a simple scan of the text reveals that Jesus was praying for Himself, His disciples (that is, the original 11 who remained faithful and were called to carry on His teaching and work on earth after He was gone), and His church.

It isn't enough, however, to know *who* Jesus was praying for. We also need to know *what* He was praying for. This is slightly less obvious for us, but it isn't because Jesus isn't clear or the text is confusing. Rather, it's because most American Christians don't spend the time needed to really meditate and soak in the word of God for it to have its intended effect. More often than we would like to admit, our temptation is to treat God's Word like a diet pill rather than a nutrition plan. We want a simple, easy fix to a blatant problem, but we aren't willing to put in the time required for real, lasting change.

However, when we pause long enough to really listen to this prayer, we see that Jesus prays specifically for five things:

1. Jesus asks God to glorify Him (v. 1, 5);
2. Jesus asks God to keep His disciples "from the evil one" and to do so "in your name, which you have given me" (v. 11, 15);
3. Jesus asks God to sanctify His disciples in the truth of God's Word (v. 17);
4. Jesus asks God to give His church the same unity He has with the Father (v. 20-21); &
5. Jesus asks God for His people to be with Him in glory (v. 24).

In other words, Jesus asks God to glorify Him by keeping His people from the evil one in the power of His name, sanctifying them by the power of His Word, giving them the same unity with one another that Jesus has with His Father, and ultimately bringing them into the glorious presence of God with Jesus Himself. Just to know that this is what Jesus is asking for in His final days...to be reminded that these are the things that are most important to Him...should lead us to repentance as we evaluate our own priorities even as it strengthens our faith in who Christ is and all that He's accomplished for us. However, to get the full picture, we have to take the next step and ask why Jesus was praying for these things.

Why Jesus Prayed

When we ask "Why did Jesus pray for these things?" we need to understand that there are two ways to answer that question:

1. The first answer can be found in what are known as Ground Clauses. Ground Clauses answer the "why" question with a "because of / since _____" response. For example, in v. 1, Jesus asks the Father to "glorify your Son." Why? "Since you have given Him authority over all flesh, to give eternal life to all whom you have given Him." (v. 2) In other words, the request is grounded in an already established reality which leads Jesus to pray in confidence.

2. The second answer to the "why" question is found in what are known as Purpose Clauses.

Rather than offering a "because of / since _____" response, Purpose Clauses give us a "so that _____" response. Looking back at v. 1, when Jesus asks the Father to glorify the Son, His purpose is so "that the Son may glorify you."

Here I want to focus on the Purpose Clauses in Jesus' prayer because as we do, we get to peek over the precipice of God's promises and get a glimpse into the glorious vista that is the eternal purpose of God for His people. As the prayer unfolds, there are four Purpose Clauses spread throughout that give a clearly defined shape to the entire structure and show us what Jesus is most passionate about.

Purpose #1 | "That the Son may glorify you." (v. 1)
First and foremost, the purpose driving Jesus' prayer was that He would be able to fully glorify His Father. There was a commitment to worship the Father as He deserved that drove the Son to full surrender and obedience to all His Father asked of Him.

Purpose #2 | "That they may be one, even as we are one." (v. 11)

Second only to His commitment to worship the Father, Jesus was committed to the community of His people. His prayer for them is that as a result of His life, death, and resurrection, they would experience the same unity with one another that He has with God in the power of His Spirit.

Purpose #3 | "So that the world may believe that you sent me." (v. 21, 23)

Third, Jesus' commitment to worship and community would be incomplete if He did not pray also for the completion of the mission He came to earth to accomplish. Thus, as His people join Him in glorifying the Father and enjoying reconciled community with one another, they participate in His mission by being an undeniable testimony of the power of the gospel to a watching world.

Purpose #4 | "To see my glory that you have given me because you loved me before the foundation of the world." (v. 24)

Fourth, Jesus knew and prayed that all these things would lead ultimately to His people beholding His glory in the presence of the Father for all eternity after He accomplishes all these purposes in and through them.

Even in such a brief survey, we can see that what matters most to Jesus are Worship, Community, and Mission, all of which lead His people into His presence for His glory and our joy as He invites us to share with Him in the Father's perfect love. If we lack in any of these three areas, or even if we prioritize them wrongly, we will fail to be the church as Jesus intends and instead become a mere caricature of what we're designed by God to be. Because of this, we want to make sure we have strategies in place as the local church to help us prioritize what Jesus prayed for and to help us live for what Jesus died for. What this means is that we must be committed to pursuing all of these together in regular rhythms of Gathering, Growing, and Going.

Worship | Gathering Together
As we saw in chapter 1, a thriving relationship with Christ is at the core of every other relationship in our lives. Because this is true, God has charged us in His Word to "consider how to stir up one another to love

and good works, not neglecting to meet together, as is the habit of some, but encouraging one another, and all the more as you see the Day drawing near." (Hebrews 10:24-25)

Each time the church gathers to worship Jesus, three things are happening:

- <u>Modeling</u>

    Jesus taught that "true worshipers will worship the Father in spirit and truth, for the Father is seeking such people to worship him. God is spirit, and those who worship him must worship in spirit and truth." John 4:23-24) The problem is that while all who believe God's Word would accept this as a true statement, this does not imply they know what it means to actually do it. Therefore, one of the primary functions of gathering together is to model for (and remind) one another what it means to worship in spirit and in truth. We do this as we receive God's Word as the highest and final authority.

    We do this as we rest in the truth and grace of the gospel Jesus lived, died, and rose again to guarantee for us. We do this as we respond to all that God promises to do and be for us in Jesus with praise, thanksgiving, repentance, and faith. And we do this as we commit together to take this good news with us into all our spheres of influence as the called out people of God, sent into the world with His message of hope and reconciliation.

- Training

As we model true worship in spirit and truth and invite others to join with us, we are at the same time training them both by direct application as well as indirect example. Therefore, we believe that it isn't enough to teach true things from Scripture if we don't help others learn what it means to live differently in light of that truth or if we don't help them learn how to engage with God directly through His Word for themselves. Similarly, we believe that it isn't enough to only pray for those in need if we don't help them learn to pray for themselves. This is essential because the church isn't a dispenser of religious services, but a training facility where pastors fulfill their calling to "equip the saints for the work of the ministry." (Ephesians 4:12)

- Sending

    Once equipped, there will be an outward thrust to compel God's people to action. As such, each time we gather, we must view the gathering as a revolving door through which we enter in order to be built up and sent out with fresh vision and renewed passion for the mission of Jesus. We gather to remember and rest in the finished work of Christ. We are sent as God's people into God's world to advance God's kingdom because while work for Christ can never lead to rest in Christ, it is just as true that rest in Christ must always lead to work for Christ.

Community | Growing Together

As important as it is for God's people to gather for worship, the community Jesus calls us to cultivate cannot be accomplished shoulder to shoulder once a week. If we want to be obedient to the "one another" commands of Scripture (like "forgive one another," "bear one another's burdens," "serve one another," and "confess your sins to one another"), it will require us to intentionally pursue gospel-centered relationships face to face with our brothers and sisters in Christ.

There isn't a single right way to accomplish this, but one thing is clear: we must be committed to building a culture of intentionally gospel-centered relationships or we will never become the church Jesus designed and desires for us to be. To build this culture, then, we need to pursue both wide community and deep community.

- Wide Community
  Wide community happens every time people gather with the express intention of getting to know one another better but where factors such as group size or the presence of new people prevent vulnerability. To be clear, this is not a bad thing. In fact, to force vulnerability in these settings is usually a sign of immaturity rather than growth. The purpose of wide community, then, is to help facilitate introductions and give people natural contexts in which to form new friendships. And because every real friendship begins with an introduction, this is a service we can and should provide as the church if we want to build healthy, lasting, thriving relationships.

- Deep Community

  Deep community, on the other hand, happens when smaller groups meet with the express intention of knowing and being known by one another at a personal level. At our church, we call these groups "Knots," which is a literary term that means "a small, tightly packed group of people." The goal of our Knots is to make discipleship not just accessible, but actual, in the lives of all of our people. To that end: we keep Knots small so that nobody can hide and everyone can be known; we keep Knots consistent so that people have time to build genuine relationships; and we keep Knots flexible so that we're always ready for multiplication as Jesus grows His church. As we do this, we grow to know, love, and follow Jesus together by His grace at a deeper and more profound level than we are able to accomplish in either the worship gathering or in the context of wide community.

Mission | Going Together

To be intentional in making disciples means we are helping others know, love, and follow Jesus with us. When we have the shared starting point of a common faith in Jesus, it's an opportunity to grow in community (like we just saw). But Jesus doesn't just call us to help other Christians grow...He calls us to join Him on His mission of saving sinners for the glory of God (see 1 Timothy 1:15-17).

- Identify

  To do this, we must first identify where others stand in relation to Jesus and His gospel. As we will discuss in the following chapters, there are three possible postures of unbelief and it's helpful to evaluate where any given person is starting in order to help them take the next step in knowing, loving, and following Jesus.

- Invest

  When Jesus gave us the Great Commission, He was giving us a call to action. It's a call to everyday mission. It's a call to invest in the lives of those who don't yet know Jesus so that we can introduce them to the grace, truth, love, life, and joy that can only be found in relationship with Him.

- <u>Invite</u>
  When confronted with the truth and grace of the gospel, the Bible doesn't allow for neutrality. In other words, the gospel demands response: we must all either embrace Jesus in humble faith or reject Jesus in selfish pride. Therefore, as we identify and invest in others, we must clearly invite them to respond in faith and obedience to the gospel and be committed to helping them as they wrestle through their questions in light of God's revealed truth.

Here again we come to the commitments that are essential to all true gospel movement:

1. We must Pray because only Jesus can save.
2. We must Pursue those who don't yet know Jesus because everyday mission doesn't happen in passing, but in the context of real relationships where we can share joys, struggles, dreams, goals, plans, and life.
3. We must Preach because where there's no gospel, there can be no salvation.
4. We must Practice what we preach because how we live the gospel says just as much about Jesus as our words.

Everyday mission doesn't happen by accident, so if we're going to engage our culture with the gospel, we must build intentionally gospel-centered relationships (with those outside the church as well as inside) so that we can love those Jesus loves, serve those Jesus serves, and tell all who will listen the saving gospel of our Savior.

DISCUSS

1. Where are you resistant to the reality that we can only follow Jesus faithfully if we are "pursuing Him together with His people" (pg. 68)? How has this impacted your growth in the gospel?

2. How do the things Jesus prayed for (pg. 73) lead you to repentance and faith? How should they?

3. What problems come when we lack any of the 3 priorities of Jesus (i.e. Worship, Community, & Mission)? What happens when either Community or Mission displaces Worship as our primary purpose?

4. Where do you see your need for Modeling, Training, & Sending? What step(s) can you take right now to prepare to receive these most effectively as you gather with God's people?

5. Are you better at building Wide Community or Deep Community? Why are both important?

6. Which of these core commitments (pg. 84) provide your greatest opportunity for making disciples?

Chapter 5

Pro-Gospel

On the night Jesus was betrayed, He had a razor-sharp focus on what mattered most, and in His "High Priestly Prayer" (John 17), Jesus asks the Father to give His church three gifts: worship, community, and mission. In doing so, He makes it clear that worship and community are not enough by themselves. If the church stops short of the mission of Jesus, then we are unfaithful to the call of Jesus, no matter how well we may believe we are doing the other two.

This is because worship and community, when experienced as Jesus prays for them to be, will always lead to the mission He's asking the Father to accomplish through His people.

But even for those of us who are most convinced of the necessity of being "missional," it is far too common for us to stop short of the actual mission of Jesus and hide behind some form of the excuse: "I don't know how."

- "I don't know how to answer the questions I'll get."
- "I don't know how to move from 'normal' conversation to 'spiritual' conversation."
- "I don't know how to ask questions that seem natural instead of forced."
- "I don't know how to share the good news of Jesus without sounding like a salesman."

As Christians, we desire to obey the Great Commission. We want to share the gospel with the people we love but so often it feels like we just don't know how to do that. We have to be careful here, however, because there's an important distinction to be made between "honest ignorance" and "intentional ignorance." Honest ignorance is a genuine lack of knowledge or skill, and when this is the primary issue, the greatest need is simple instruction and training. Intentional ignorance, on the other hand, is not merely a lack of knowledge/skill, but a purposeful avoidance of them in order to sidestep the responsibility they inevitably lay on us.

We may not always be able to identify clearly whether we're battling honest or intentional ignorance, but whenever we see that we've stopped short of the mission of Jesus, the invitation of the gospel is to openly and humbly confess our ignorance, repent of our disobedience, and ask God for grace to follow Jesus into mission, not just into worship and community.

Mission in the Early Church

After His resurrection, before Jesus ascended to the Father and sent the Holy Spirit at Pentecost, He met with His followers in Jerusalem and told them: "You will receive power when the Holy Spirit has come upon you, and you will be my witnesses in Jerusalem and in all Judea and Samaria, and to the ends of the earth." (Acts 1:8)

As the book of Acts unfolds, we see Him keeping this promise and building His church, in the power of the Holy Spirit, through the faithful obedience of His people:

- In Acts 2, Jesus kept His promise to send the Holy Spirit and He used Peter to take His gospel to thousands at Pentecost.
- In Acts 3, Jesus continued to heal the sick and His followers used that opportunity to testify to the name of Christ.
- In Acts 4, Jesus gave His followers boldness to face down the religious and political elite and boldly speak the truth of God in the face of opposition.
- In Acts 5, we see the opposition forming to the church of Jesus: both from the outside and from the inside.
- In Acts 6-7, that opposition turns into full-on persecution as Stephen is stoned to death for preaching the gospel of Jesus Christ, and Luke tells us in Acts 8:1 that "There arose on that day a great persecution against the church in Jerusalem, and they were all scattered throughout the regions of Judea and Samaria, except the apostles."

Then in Acts 8-9, as this first wave of persecution reaches its peak and the church is scattered, Luke tells us in Acts 8:4 that "those who were scattered went about preaching the word." They had heard the gospel. They had believed the gospel. They loved Jesus and they were willing to follow Him wherever He led them, even if it meant they were going to suffer. So as their homes, jobs, and families were taken from them, no one could take away the gospel, which meant no one could keep them from following Jesus.

As they followed Jesus on His mission to the world, Luke begins to give us clear examples of how the world responded. He does it by telling us three specific salvation stories among the thousands he could have reported.

In the first half of Acts 8 we read about a magician named Simon. In the second half of Acts 8, he reports the salvation of the Ethiopian Eunuch (which we'll discuss in chapter 6). And finally, in Acts 9, we see the salvation of Saul (which we'll discuss in chapter 7).

As we dig into these stories, we can begin to see why Luke picked each one and what the Holy Spirit intends for us to learn from them.

In chapter 2, we saw that maturing as disciples of Jesus means growing to know, love, and follow Him more. Discipleship is living the Gospel Cycle:
- The more we know Jesus, the more we love Him.
- The more we love Jesus, the more we follow Him.
- The more we follow Jesus, the more we know Him. [Repeat]

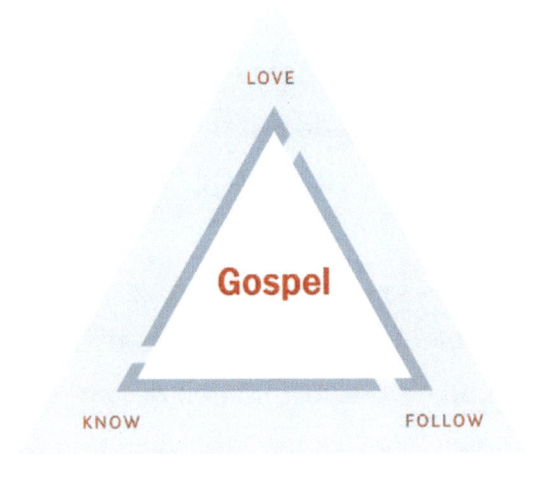

This Gospel Cycle is what it looks like to walk with Jesus for a lifetime. It also gives us simple, practical ways to think and talk about what's going well and where we need to grow in any given season of our lives. But what about those who don't yet believe the gospel? What about our friends, neighbors, and family members who have never heard of Jesus? Or those who hate Jesus? Or those who say they're Christians but their lives just don't match up with what they say?

This is where the Gospel Cycle becomes even more practical because knowing, loving, and following Jesus aren't just our core needs as believers. Rather, these are actually the fundamental needs we all have as human beings created in the image of God. That being said, we need to understand that not all unbelief looks and sounds the same. Since that's true, if we want to follow Jesus on His mission, then we need to learn to identify where others are starting from in order to invest in them and invite them to respond to the gospel most effectively.

ANTI-GOSPEL

LOVE

Gospel

KNOW　　　　　FOLLOW

PRE-GOSPEL　　　　　PRO-GOSPEL

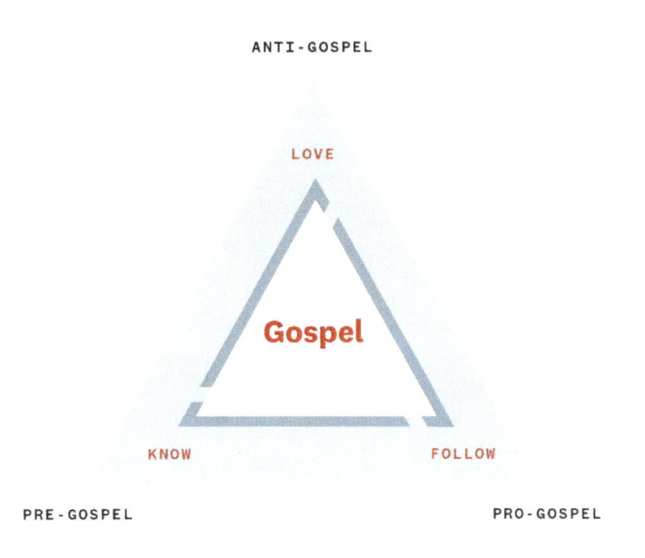

IDENTIFY | Pro-Gospel Description

As you can see in the diagram above, when we understand discipleship as growing in the Gospel Cycle, it becomes clear that there are three possible postures of unbelief:

1. Pre-Gospel;
2. Anti-Gospel;
3. Pro-Gospel.

As we dig deeper into the salvation stories of Acts 8-9, we find the same thing there, and the first one Luke highlights is "Pro-Gospel."

He does this by telling us the dramatic story of a local magician named Simon.

Starting in Acts 8:9, Luke tells us that "there was a man named Simon, who had previously practiced magic in the city and amazed the people of Samaria, saying that he himself was somebody great. [10] They all paid attention to him, from the least to the greatest, saying, "This man is the power of God that is called Great." [11] And they paid attention to him because for a long time he had amazed them with his magic. [12] But when they believed Philip as he preached good news about the kingdom of God and the name of Jesus Christ, they were baptized, both men and women. [13] Even Simon himself believed, and after being baptized he continued with Philip. And seeing signs and great miracles performed, he was amazed."

For his readers in the first century, this would have been the equivalent of later generations being told that Mohammed or Buddha put their faith in Jesus and surrendered their lives to Him as their one, true King. Evidently, Simon was famous in that region.

Through tricks and what was likely demonic activity interpreted as magic, he had deceived the people of Samaria to the point that they all agreed that he was "the power of God that is called Great." (v. 10)

So when Philip came and preached the gospel and the people turned from Simon to Jesus, it was a big deal that Simon didn't fight for power but actually joined them, as Luke says: "Even Simon himself believed, and after being baptized he continued with Philip. And seeing signs and great miracles performed, he was amazed."

Simon knew real power when he saw it and he was willing to admit that this was different than the magic he'd been using to deceive the people. The question, though, was whether this was going to be merely a change in his rhetoric or a change in his life? Was this just a change of action or also a genuine change of heart?

Luke doesn't leave us hanging for long, as he goes onto answer our question beginning in v. 14: "[14] Now when the apostles at Jerusalem heard that Samaria had received the word of God, they sent to them

Peter and John, [15] who came down and prayed for them that they might receive the Holy Spirit, [16] for he had not yet fallen on any of them, but they had only been baptized in the name of the Lord Jesus. [17] Then they laid their hands on them and they received the Holy Spirit. [18] Now when Simon saw that the Spirit was given through the laying on of the apostles' hands, he offered them money, [19] saying, "Give me this power also, so that anyone on whom I lay my hands may receive the Holy Spirit." [20] But Peter said to him, "May your silver perish with you, because you thought you could obtain the gift of God with money. [21] You have neither part nor lot in this matter, for your heart is not right before God. [22] Repent, therefore, of this wickedness of yours, and pray to the Lord that, if possible, the intent of your heart may be forgiven you. [23] For I see that you are in the gall of bitterness and in the bond of iniquity.'"

What becomes clear as Luke continues the story is that even though Simon claimed to believe; even though he'd been baptized; even though he was giving all the initial, external signs of conversion; none of that guaranteed genuine heart change.

And by the grace of God, Peter was able to see through the facade and call this man to real repentance.

What we see in Simon is a posture of unbelief we call "Pro-Gospel." People in this "Pro-Gospel" category:

- Tend to have a very positive view of the church or of Christianity, but it's mixed with a confusion about what the gospel really is and what it means to surrender all of life to Jesus as King.

- "Pro-Gospel" people have heard the truth of Jesus and embraced it intellectually. There can even be excitement about the gospel because it fits with and promotes something they really care about like a moral or political position, or simply a traditional value system.

In Acts 8, while Simon outwardly acknowledged Jesus, his true motivation was exposed when he offered to buy the gift of the Spirit. In that one act, Simon displayed that he was still craving the power he once had and he wanted to use the gospel to get it.

Those, like Simon, who assume such a "Pro-Gospel" posture aren't genuinely seeking the crucified, risen, reigning Jesus who demands their whole lives and deserves their worship. Instead, they are seeking a caricature of Jesus who serves their needs and supports their causes.

In our context today, this is what we might call the "Christian subculture." Churches are full of this form of unbelief and no church is immune to it. But it can be so hard to see clearly because it's an attempt to identify outwardly with what makes us look righteous or godly, while being content with no real heart change. What it really comes down to is trying to say that "*Jesus is my Savior from sin*" without having to say "*Jesus is Lord of my life and all I have and all I am belongs to Him.*"

The core need of those in this "Pro-Gospel" stage is to follow Jesus, and what's striking about Peter's response to Simon is that he was able to cut through the external things that looked so good and really get to the heart.

Peter was brave enough to challenge Simon's words when they didn't match his life, and he was secure enough to risk a bad reputation by refusing to remain silent, because he believed Jesus when He said: "If you love me, you will keep my commandments." (John 14:15)

INVEST | Pro-Gospel Need

Again, the reason we need to learn to identify where others are starting from is so that we can more effectively invest in them and invite them to respond to the gospel of Jesus.

So how can you know if you're able to effectively engage your "Pro-Gospel" friends and family with the truth and grace of Jesus? Well, you can begin by asking yourself two diagnostic questions:

1. Do I know the Scriptures well enough to see when they aren't being believed?
2. Do I know people well enough to challenge them when this happens?

Your next step of investment will look different depending on how you answer these questions.

If you can't say "Yes" to #2, then your priority needs to be pursuing intentionally gospel-centered relationships as we discussed in chapter 1.

If you can't say "Yes" to #1, then your priority needs to be familiarizing yourself with the gospel as it is revealed in the Word of God. This may mean committing to a Scripture Reading Plan, inviting a friend to join you, asking for accountability, and praying for God to change your heart. More than this, however, a "No" on #1 could indicate that you are in the "Pro-Gospel" category yourself. If you are concerned that this may be true of you, this is a perfect opportunity to be vulnerable with a trusted brother or sister in Jesus and ask them to help you discern God's voice.

[NOTE: If you would like help in taking this step, see Appendix 1 | The Gift of Repentance.]

PRO-GOSPEL SUMMARY

ANTI-GOSPEL

LOVE

Gospel

KNOW FOLLOW

PRE-GOSPEL PRO-GOSPEL

DESCRIPTION

- Inaccurate knowledge of the gospel, positive view of the Church/Christianity.
- Has heard the truth of Jesus and embraced it. There is an approval of, sometimes even an excitement about, the gospel due to various positive associations, ranging from endorsement of political views to promotion of preferred moral stances.
- People in this posture of unbelief are not accepting Jesus as Lord so much as embracing a caricature of Jesus who serves their needs and supports their causes.
- This is the Christian subculture.

NEED

- The core need of those in this posture of unbelief is to FOLLOW Jesus.
- Jesus told His followers: "If you love me, you will keep my commandments." (John 14:15)
- As Christians, we have the privilege and the responsibility of finding our deepest joy in full surrender to Jesus as Lord and King and inviting others to do the same. We must never be content with agreement without obedience!

DISCUSS

1. What is your go-to excuse for NOT sharing the gospel? In what way(s) does this reveal "intentional ignorance"?

2. Is the idea that "not all unbelief looks and sounds the same" (pg. 93) new to you? How should it shape our posture toward and responses to those who don't yet believe the gospel?

3. How are you tempted to try to use Jesus to support your cause/agenda instead of fully surrendering it to Jesus as Lord?

4. Where are you resistant to the idea that "we need to learn to identify where others are starting from so that we can more effectively invest in them" (pg. 100)? Why is it necessary?

5. Share your answers to the diagnostic questions on pg. 100 & how you've seen them in your life.

6. Re-read the Pro-Gospel Summary (pg. 102-103): What's new? What's confusing? What's hard? What's exciting?

Chapter 6

Pre-Gospel

As we saw in chapter 5, the first posture of unbelief Luke highlights in Acts 8-9 is "Pro-Gospel." Following this, he then turns his attention to a clear example of what we're calling "Pre-Gospel."

To unpack this for us, Luke shares the story of the Ethiopian Eunuch. Beginning in Acts 8:26, he tells us: "[26] Now an angel of the Lord said to Philip, "Rise and go toward the south to the road that goes down from Jerusalem to Gaza." This is a desert place.

> ²⁷ And he rose and went. And there was an Ethiopian, a eunuch, a court official of Candace, queen of the Ethiopians, who was in charge of all her treasure. He had come to Jerusalem to worship ²⁸ and was returning, seated in his chariot, and he was reading the prophet Isaiah."

From this brief description, we're able to draw out some key information about who this man was. First, we know that as a high ranking official in the Queen's court, he was a man of considerable power and influence. Second, we can infer from the fact that the Queen left him in charge of her royal treasury that he was trustworthy and had earned her respect. Third, since he was a eunuch, he was clearly willing to do whatever it took to achieve his goals, which tells us he was unswervingly committed to what mattered to him.

In addition to these characteristics, we can tell that he's searching and that he's desperate because, unsatisfied with the tribal African religions he grew up with, he was longing for more and he was willing to travel 500 miles from Ethiopia to Jerusalem in search of answers.

Not only that, but according to the Old Testament, we know that as a Gentile (even more as a eunuch) he wouldn't have been allowed into the temple, which means that after traveling hundreds of miles, he would have been turned away at the doors. So this powerful, trustworthy, committed royal official who was both searching and desperate was on his way home, no doubt still feeling the sting of disappointment.

And while he was rich enough to afford a copy of an Isaiah scroll, he had no way to understand what he read. He had never heard the good news of Jesus, so the clearest Messianic prophecies in all of Scripture didn't give him hope, they just confused him.

ANTI-GOSPEL

LOVE

Gospel

KNOW   FOLLOW

PRE-GOSPEL   PRO-GOSPEL

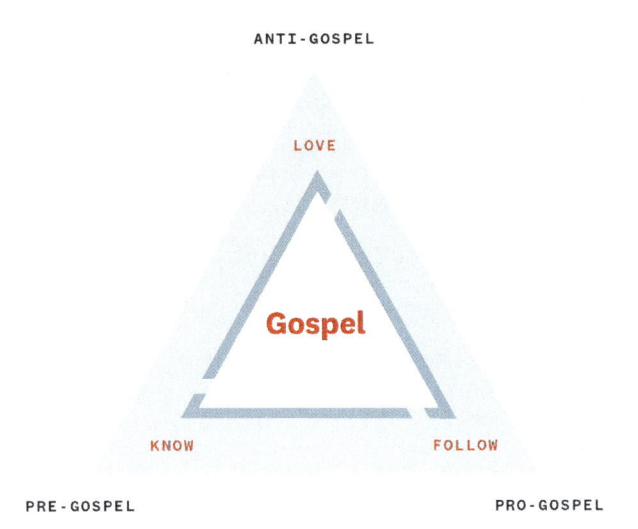

IDENTIFY | Pre-Gospel Description

This is because in every way, this Ethiopian Eunuch was "Pre-Gospel."

- He had no knowledge of the gospel;
- He had never accepted or rejected the truth of Jesus because he'd never heard it; &
- He was open to being taught, rebuked, corrected, and trained. He was seeking truth, but he didn't know where to look or who to ask for help.

The beautiful thing here is that even though this Ethiopian Eunuch didn't yet know Jesus, Jesus knew him and He was pursuing this man through Philip.

The Holy Spirit was working. He was drawing the Ethiopian Eunuch and what he needed, more than anything, was for someone to simply and clearly tell him about Jesus. Ultimately, this is the core need for all who fit this "Pre-Gospel" posture.

As surprising as it may seem to those who grew up attending church or in close association with those who did, this "Pre-Gospel" posture of unbelief is becoming more and more common in our culture. This should not come as a shock, however, when we consider [a recent Barna study (2018)](#) which showed that over 50% of church attenders had never heard of the Great Commission, and another 25% said it sounded familiar but they didn't know what it was.

If this number represents the church across America, then it follows that those who do not know the Great Commission will not fulfill the Great Commission. As the apostle Paul said it in Romans 10:14-15, "How then will they call on him in whom they have not believed? And how are they to believe in him of whom they have never heard? And how are they to hear without someone preaching? And how are they to preach unless they are sent?"

INVEST | Pre-Gospel Need

For those who do know the Great Commission, we understand that all followers of Jesus have already been sent. And when Jesus sent us, He gave us His Spirit and His Word, He promised His presence, and He did all this with ultimate authority. And yet, in unbelief and disobedience, we have in large part neglected the outward-facing mission of Jesus and settled for inward-facing retreat from the world. In fact, we have come to a place in our culture where it is becoming more and more common that the people we interact with on a daily basis have no knowledge of Jesus, the gospel, or the Bible to any extent at all, and if we're honest, we have to acknowledge that this is our fault, not theirs.

As a result, the church has two options:
1. We can see this as a defeat and mourn the collapse of "Christendom."
2. Or we can repent of our unbelief and disobedience and choose to see this as an opportunity. Only then will we be ready, able, and willing to share the gospel in creative and powerful ways that we've never had the opportunity to before?

People all around us are searching and they're desperate, just like the Ethiopian Eunuch. And just like him, they're wide open if we're ready to go when the Holy Spirit says "go." Just look what happened with Philip: "29 And the Spirit said to Philip, "Go over and join this chariot." 30 So Philip ran to him and heard him reading Isaiah the prophet and asked, "Do you understand what you are reading?" 31 And he said, "How can I, unless someone guides me?" And he invited Philip to come up and sit with him. 32 Now the passage of the Scripture that he was reading was this: *Like a sheep he was led to the slaughter, and like a lamb before its shearer is silent, so he opens not his mouth.* 33 *In his humiliation justice was denied him. Who can describe his generation? For his life is taken away from the earth.*

34 And the eunuch said to Philip, "About whom, I ask you, does the prophet say this, about himself or about someone else?" 35 Then Philip opened his mouth, and beginning with this Scripture he told him the good news about Jesus. 36 And as they were going along the road they came to some water, and the eunuch said, "See, here is water. What prevents me from being baptized?" 38 And he commanded the

> chariot to stop, and they both went down into the water, Philip and the eunuch, and he baptized him."

In all of this, God is the one drawing the Ethiopian. God is the one working on his heart. God is the one orchestrating this entire conversation, not Philip. What, then, was Philip's role? The simple answer is: Philip was ready. His life was structured in such a way that when the Spirit told him to go, he was ready and he went without question, complaint, or hesitation because he knew there were people all around him who had never heard the name of Jesus and he wasn't willing to sit back and hope that somebody else would tell them.

As followers of Jesus, we have both the privilege and the responsibility of sharing His gospel with those who have never heard it. On its face, that seems like a relatively simple proposition, but how often do we overcomplicate it? How often do we buy into the lie that if we can't do it perfectly, then we shouldn't do it at all? How often do we battle feelings of inadequacy and ignorance, and spend so much time focused on ourselves that we lose sight of Jesus and stop following Him on His mission?

But if we know Jesus and we have people in our lives who have never heard His name or understood His gospel, then what matters most isn't whether or not we're perfectly prepared, have the exact right words, the ideal strategy, or the most compelling presentation. No, what matters is whether or not we're willing and ready (like Philip) to preach the good news of Jesus to our "Pre-Gospel" friends and family in terms they can understand and relate to.

Bearing Fruit

So what do we do if we discover this to be true of us? First, we need to honestly admit where we are, not only to God but also to Christian brothers and sisters we trust. We shouldn't be timid about acknowledging this because the simple fact is that while Jesus calls us all to make disciples, He's calling others to make disciples of us at the same time. In other words, we need the gospel as much as everyone else.

In reality, we will never experience the depths of His grace until we acknowledge the depths of our need, and this applies just as much to this struggle as to any other.

Second, we need to lean into the life Jesus died to give us. In John 15, Jesus tells His followers that He is the vine and we are the branches. He shows us that we will never bear fruit unless we get connected and stay connected to Him because He is the source of our life in God. He gives us this life by giving us His Spirit, through whom He promises both fruit and gifts.

Cultivation | Fruit of the Spirit
Jesus, the True Vine, doesn't just command us to bear fruit. Rather, He sends His Spirit to work in and through us to accomplish all that He requires and provide all that He expects of us. When He does, the apostle Paul tells us in Galatians 5:22-23 that "the fruit of the Spirit is love, joy, peace, patience, kindness, goodness, faithfulness, gentleness, and self-control."

In other words, the life of the Christian is a life that reflects this fruit of the Spirit and is becoming more and more defined by these characteristics. If you can't say you're ready or willing to offer the hope of the gospel to those who have never experienced it, the place to start is by evaluating your own life and honestly asking whether or not these things are true of you. If you aren't sure, there are two steps you can take:

1. First, ask God to show you where you aren't bearing the fruit of the Spirit and trust His grace and promises to give you all that He commands.

2. Second, as mentioned above, ask others where they see these characteristics in you and be encouraged by their answers. Then ask them where they see a lack of these characteristics and be challenged to press into the mercy of Jesus, "the author and perfecter of your faith." (Hebrews 12:2)

Expectation | Gifts of the Spirit

As we seek to cultivate the fruit of the Spirit, we can do so in hope because in Romans 12:6-8, 1 Corinthians 12, and 1 Peter 4:7-11, the Bible teaches that all Christians have been given gifts by the Holy Spirit for the glory of God and the building up of the body of Christ (which is the church).

Because that's true, we can eagerly expect the Holy Spirit to not just work in us (bearing fruit) but to work through us (as we use His gifts) to accomplish His purpose of glorifying the Father and the Son. If you already know what gifts the Spirit has given you, now is the time to share that with your pastors and ask them how you can best partner with your local church to be as effective as God intends for you to be.

However, if you don't yet know what gifts the Spirit has given you, then this may be one of the most important and exciting things you have ever done as a follower of Jesus. As you read through the following descriptions (adapted from the [Ministry Tools Resource Center](#)), evaluate with two questions in mind:

1. Where have I seen these in my life as a follower of Jesus?
2. Would the people who know me best agree with my answers?

SPIRITUAL GIFTS

- **Administration** (1 Corinthians 12:28)
  To steer the body toward the accomplishment of God-given goals and directives by planning, organizing, and supervising others.

- **Apostle** (Ephesians 4:11; 1 Corinthians 12:28)
  To be sent forth to new frontiers with the gospel, providing leadership over church bodies and maintaining authority over spiritual matters pertaining to the church.

- **Discernment** (1 Corinthians 12:10)
  To clearly distinguish truth from error by judging whether the behavior or teaching is from God, Satan, human error, or human power.

- **Evangelism** (Ephesians 4:11)
  To bear uncommon fruit as a messenger of the good news of the Gospel.

- **Exhortation** (Romans 12:8)
  To use words of comfort and counsel to help others know, love, & follow Jesus.

- **Faith** (1 Corinthians 12:8-10)

  To be firmly persuaded of God's power and promises to accomplish His will and to display such a confidence in His Word that circumstances/obstacles do not shake that conviction.

- **Giving** (Romans 12:8)

  To share what material resources you have with liberality and cheerfulness without thought of return.

- **Healing** (1 Corinthians 12:9, 28-30)

  To be used as a means through which God makes people whole: physically, emotionally, mentally, or spiritually.

- **Helps** (1 Corinthians 12:28)

  To render support or assistance to others in the body so as to free them up for ministry.

- **Hospitality** (1 Peter 4:9-10)

  To warmly welcome people, even strangers, into one's home or church with gospel purpose.

- **Knowledge** (1 Corinthians 12:8)
  To seek to learn as much about the Bible as possible through the gathering of information and the analyzing of data.

- **Leadership** (Romans 12:8)
  To stand before the people in such a way as to attend to the direction of the body with such care and diligence so as to motivate others to get involved in the accomplishment of these goals.

- **Mercy** (Romans 12:8)
  To be sensitive toward those who are suffering (whether physically, mentally, or emotionally) so as to feel genuine sympathy with their misery, speaking words of compassion and caring for them with deeds of love to help alleviate their distress.

- **Miracles** (1 Corinthians 12:10, 28)
  To be enabled by God to perform mighty deeds which witnesses acknowledge to be of supernatural origin and means.

- **Pastor** (Ephesians 4:11)
  To be responsible for spiritually caring for, protecting, guiding, equipping, and feeding a group of believers entrusted to one's care.

- **Prophecy** (Romans 12:6; 1 Corinthians 12:10; Ephesians 4:11)
  To speak forth the message of God to/for His people.

- **Service** (Romans 12:7)
  To identify undone tasks in God's work, however menial, and use available resources to get the job done.

- **Teaching** (Romans 12:7; 1 Corinthians 12:28; Ephesians 4:11)
  To instruct others in the Bible in a logical, systematic way so as to communicate pertinent information for true understanding and growth.

- **Tongues** (1 Corinthians 12:10; 14:27-28)
  To speak in a language not previously learned so unbelievers can hear God's message in their own language or the body be edified.

- **Interpretation of Tongues**
  (1 Corinthians 12:10; 14:27-28)
  To translate the message of someone who has spoken in tongues.

- **Wisdom** (1 Corinthians 12:8)
  To apply knowledge to life in such a way as to make spiritual truths quite relevant and practical in proper decision-making and daily life situations.

If you find yourself hesitant or you feel unequipped to preach the gospel of Jesus to those who have never heard, your starting point needs to be to recenter on cultivation and expectation, bearing the fruit of the Spirit and using the gifts of the Spirit in humble confidence that in the gospel, you have all that you need to be faithful to all that God asks of you.

[NOTE: If you would like a refresher on what the gospel is, see Appendix 2 | The Gospel.]

PRE-GOSPEL SUMMARY

ANTI-GOSPEL

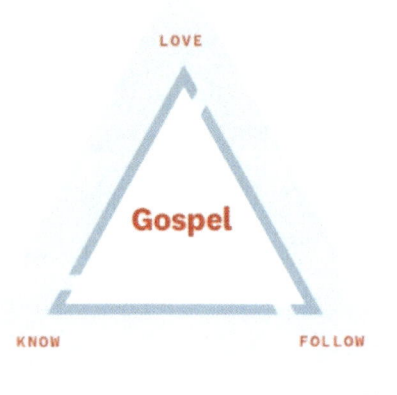

LOVE

Gospel

KNOW FOLLOW

PRE-GOSPEL PRO-GOSPEL

DESCRIPTION

- No knowledge of the gospel.
- Has neither accepted nor rejected the truth of Jesus because they have never heard it. There is no animosity toward or bias against the gospel be use there are no negative or positive associations made at all with Christianity and/or the Church.
- This includes unreached people groups, but increasingly describes American culture in which parents, schools, and peers have not only no belief in Jesus but also no exposure to the Church, the gospel, or the Bible.

NEED

- The core need of those in this posture of unbelief is to KNOW Jesus.
- Romans 10:14 reminds us: "How then will they call on Him in whom they have not believed? And how are they to believe in Him of whom they have never heard? And how are they to hear without someone preaching?"
- As Christians, we have the privilege and the responsibility of sharing the good news of Jesus with those who have never heard it.

DISCUSS

1. Where have you encountered this Pre-Gospel posture of unbelief (in yourself or others)? How are spiritual conversations with people in this category refreshing/unique/difficult?

2. "Those who do not know the Great Commission will not fulfill the Great Commission." (pg. 109)
   –How does this challenge you?
   –Where does it expose need for growth?

3. Do you see the growing lack of gospel knowledge in our culture as primarily a defeat or an opportunity? How does/should this shape your response to it?

4. How are you tempted to get distracted or dissuaded from sharing the gospel by overcomplicating it (see pg. 112)? What helps you recenter on the simple, clear gospel?

5. Where in your life do you see the fruit & gifts of the Spirit? Where do you need to grow in both?

6. Re-read the Pre-Gospel Summary (pg. 122-123): What's new? What's confusing? What's hard? What's exciting?

Chapter 7

Anti-Gospel

As we've already seen, there are three postures of unbelief Luke showcases for us in Acts 8-9. We've already looked at "Pro-Gospel" and "Pre-Gospel." Now in Acts 9, Luke turns his attention to "Anti-Gospel." To bring this posture of unbelief to life, he tells us the story of his mentor, the Apostle Paul.

At the beginning of Acts 8, Luke told us that Saul approved of Stephen's execution and that he was "ravaging the church, and entering house after house, he dragged off men and women and committed them to prison." (Acts 8:3)

As he continues in Acts 9, we see that nothing has changed. Luke says: "But Saul, still breathing threats and murder against the disciples of the Lord, went to the high priest 2 and asked him for letters to the synagogues at Damascus, so that if he found any belonging to the Way, men or women, he might bring them bound to Jerusalem. 3 Now as he went on his way, he approached Damascus, and suddenly a light from heaven shone around him. 4 And falling to the ground, he heard a voice saying to him, "Saul, Saul, why are you persecuting me?" 5 And he said, "Who are you, Lord?" And he said, "I am Jesus, whom you are persecuting." (Acts 8:1-4)

Saul of Tarsus - the man we now know as the Apostle Paul who wrote half the New Testament - was a man of strong passion and deep learning. He had been trained in the school of Gamaliel, and he had the highest possible pedigree for a young Israelite man. As he notes in Philippians 3:5-7, he was "circumcised on the eighth day, of the people of Israel, of the tribe of Benjamin, a Hebrew of Hebrews; as to the law, a

Pharisee; as to zeal, a persecutor of the church; as to righteousness under the law, blameless."

According to Saul and those who knew him well, he knew it all and had it all. But he was "Anti-Gospel" in every sense of the word. Based on misinformation and misunderstanding, Saul hated Jesus, he hated Christianity, and he was determined not to simply ignore the church, but to destroy it. By the grace of God, however, even as Saul was on His way to do just that, the risen Christ Himself intervened by knocking Saul to the ground, blinding him, speaking to him from heaven, and telling him what he was going to do next.

As the story unfolds, Saul does what he's told and for three days he waits, blind and confused, not knowing what will happen next. But while Saul is waiting, Jesus is still working, as Luke tells us in Acts 9:10-19: "[10] Now there was a disciple at Damascus named Ananias. The Lord said to him in a vision, "Ananias." And he said, "Here I am, Lord." [11] And the Lord said to him, "Rise and go to the street called Straight, and at the house of Judas look for a man of Tarsus named Saul, for behold, he is praying, [12] and he has seen in a vision a man named Ananias come in and lay his hands on him so that he might regain his sight." ¹³ But Ananias answered, "Lord, I have heard from many about this man, how much evil he has done to your saints at Jerusalem.

¹⁴ And here he has authority from the chief priests to bind all who call on your name." ¹⁵ But the Lord said to him, "Go, for he is a chosen instrument of mine to carry my name before the Gentiles and kings and the children of Israel. ¹⁶ For I will show him how much he must suffer for the sake of my name." ¹⁷ So Ananias departed and entered the house. And laying his hands on him he said, "Brother Saul, the Lord Jesus who appeared to you on the road by which you came has sent me so that you may regain your sight and be filled with the Holy Spirit." ¹⁸ And immediately something like scales fell from his eyes, and he regained his sight. Then he rose and was baptized; ¹⁹ and taking food, he was strengthened."

When Jesus appeared to Ananias, all He had to do was speak his name and his immediate response was "Here I am, Lord." This was a pledge of allegiance, a declaration of full surrender and submission.

He was willing to do whatever his King required of him. But even for Ananias, with that as his starting point, what Jesus tells him to do next sounds like an unreasonable command.

In fact, Ananias has to clarify that he's hearing Jesus correctly. He needed to make sure they were both talking about the same Saul: the man who was only in town because he wanted to arrest Christians and destroy the church.

Of course, Jesus had it right and He assured Ananias that they were, in fact, talking about the same Saul. In response, what Ananias models for us is simple obedience rooted in deep faith. Jesus was clear that He'd chosen Saul, and that was enough to remove all of Ananias' fears about what consequences may come if he loved Saul by going to him, served Saul by healing him, and told Saul the good news of the gospel.

Luke has many things to teach us, but one of the core lessons we need to learn here is that when you see people through a gospel lens, no one is too far gone. No one is beyond the saving work of God's strong, amazing grace. It is too easy for us write people off and assume that what they believe about God and His Word will never change, but we only make those assumptions because we don't really understand the power and purposes of God.

Saul's conversion should rebuke our small expectations of God. It should also remind us that because the grace of Jesus is powerful and His gospel is true, we should be asking and expecting God to do so much more than we are.

ANTI-GOSPEL

LOVE

Gospel

KNOW　　　　　　　FOLLOW

PRE-GOSPEL　　　　　　　PRO-GOSPEL

IDENTIFY | Anti-Gospel Description

No matter how isolated or removed we might feel at times, all of us know people whose unbelief comes out as "Anti-Gospel." What that means is:

- Whether they understand it rightly or not, they hold a negative view of the church and Christianity; &
- They've heard the truth of Jesus and rejected it. For a variety of reasons (from being treated poorly by Christians to negative cultural depictions of Christianity to a simple lack of belief in the truths taught in Scripture) they either dismiss or actively oppose Christ.

Very often, people in this category are not rejecting Jesus as much as they're rejecting a caricature of Jesus. To assume that those who know the name of Jesus also know the character of Jesus is absurd. Therefore, part of our task as disciples of Jesus is to testify to His true character and His true teaching, which is the gospel.

As we do, the fields are ripe for harvest (Luke 10:2) because "Anti-Gospel" is, without question, the dominant cultural posture in America.

- The church is marginalized by the government as a voting block.
- The church is mocked by the universities as anti-intellectual.
- The church is ridiculed by the sciences as a superstition.
- The church is reduced by the business world to nothing more than a target audience.
- The church is tolerated by society at large only so far as it observes cultural norms.

But what happens when the church operates as Jesus intended? What happens when we refuse to abide by cultural expectations and limitations placed on us and instead follow the call of Jesus to make disciples of all nations, teaching them to obey all that He commanded? What happens when we embrace our political, intellectual, ethnic, and cultural diversity and embody the gospel in *every* sphere of life? What happens when we refuse to bow out of academic, philosophical, scientific, and political conversations because we're convinced that our perspective is the one that truly maps onto the human experience most accurately and we're convinced that the world needs to hear the truth God has revealed?

Well, it is at precisely this point that the "anti-gospel" nature of our society is no longer able to be denied. It is at this point that the double-standard comes into full view. This is because the same tolerance, which for so long was demanded of the dominant culture when it was primarily influenced by the church, is no longer expected now that church's influence has decreased.

And so, the question we need to ask is: "How can we invest in a meaningful way into individuals (and into a society) who regard us as enemies for simple faithfulness to the Lordship of Jesus?"

INVEST | Anti-Gospel Need
Again, we all know people who fit the description above. For most of us, it's not true that our friends and family have never heard of Jesus or don't know anything about Him, but rather that they simply don't love Him, and that's what they need more than anything else.

The church must therefore be ready and willing to both embody and proclaim the gospel of Jesus, because if it does not infiltrate every sphere of our lives, it will never infiltrate every sphere of our society.

This means that we must refuse to be marginalized by the government, and instead the church must train and send faithful men and women into politics to testify to Christ and demonstrate how the gospel is compelling as they lead by speaking truth in love, being gracious to those with whom they disagree even as they fight for what they believe in.

This means that we must refuse to retreat when mocked or ridiculed in the academy, and instead the church must train and send faithful men and women into the universities and scientific communities to testify to Christ and demonstrate how the explanatory power, predictive power, internal consistency, rational coherence, and historical reliability of a Biblical worldview is not only competitive with, but superior to, all competing worldviews and must be taken seriously, all while praying for those who consider us enemies and testifying to the humble love of our King.

This means that we must refuse to settle for creating a subculture for our movies, art, and music and instead commit to producing the best art we are capable of because we're convinced that the best way to engage culture is to create it.

Finally, this means that we must refuse to remain silent in order to maintain the illusion of peace. Jesus commands us to be peacemakers, not peace keepers. As a result, we must be ready and willing to stand our ground, boldly proclaim the truth of the gospel, and clearly assert our perspective, all while acknowledging our tendency to error (just like everyone else) and holding to the Bible as our highest authority (our first and final appeal).

INVITE | Anti-Gospel

As we grow to know, love, and follow Jesus together by His grace and invite our "anti-gospel" neighbors to join us, we will no doubt face opposition. When this comes, we will have two options: (1) We can retreat into silence and safety; or (2) We can engage with humility and confidence, trusting that our Lord knows what He's doing and that He will lead us as a Good Shepherd.

Scripture doesn't allow us to opt for the first option, so we must prepare to follow the example of the apostles in Acts 5:41-42 who, after being beaten for preaching the gospel and warned to remain silent, "left the presence of the council, rejoicing that they were counted worthy to suffer dishonor for the name. And every day, in the temple and from house to house, they did not cease teaching and preaching that the Christ is Jesus."

As we engage culture in this kind of humble confidence, what we are always watching and praying for is the opportunity to invite others out of their opposition to Jesus and into genuine faith. To do this, however, we must understand three foundational Biblical realities:

1. What Faith Isn't;
2. What Faith Is; &
3. What Faith Does.

What Faith Isn't

We all tend to assume the best about ourselves and our motives, and many of us do the same for others. Because that's true and we naturally don't want to hurt others feelings or be unnecessarily critical, it's important for us to be clear about what faith isn't so that we won't be deceived right along those who think they believe when they really don't (or those who have become convinced that one of these alternatives is what we're inviting them into).

- *Faith isn't knowing the right answers.* | As James 2:19 tells us, "You believe that God is one; you do well. Even the demons believe - and shudder."

- *Faith isn't doing the right things.* | Paul says in Galatians 2:16 that "by works of the law no one will be justified." That is, simply obeying the rules can never be enough to make us right with God.

- *Faith isn't a desire for salvation.* | In Luke 18:18-30, a rich man came to Jesus seeking salvation, but he left unsatisfied because he wanted God's salvation on his own terms.

- *Faith isn't a fear of hell.* | This is the negative form of the previous statement. Wanting to avoid the consequences of sin isn't the same as reconciliation with a holy, gracious God.

- *Faith isn't confession.* | Pharaoh (Exodus 9:27; 10:16), Balaam (Numbers 22:34), Achan (Joshua 7:20), Saul (1 Samuel 15:24,30; 26:21), and Judas (Matthew 27:4) all said the same thing: "I have sinned." And yet they were all destroyed by the just wrath of God for their rebellion because their confession of sin was not accompanied with genuine repentance.

- *Faith isn't sorrow over sin.* | When he was confronted with the wickedness of his actions, Judas fell into a deep sorrow. Again, though, even this sorrow drove him not to repentance but to suicide (Matthew 27:3-10).

What Faith Is

Identifying what faith isn't, though, is only half the battle. We must be on guard for counterfeits, but if we don't know what we're looking for, we'll never be able to lead others into genuine faith. So what is faith? In the Bible, the closest we come to a simple definition of faith is found in Hebrews: "Now faith is the assurance of things hoped for, the conviction of things not seen. And without it is impossible to please [God], for whoever would draw near to God must believe that He exists and that He rewards those who earnestly seek Him." (Hebrews 11:1,6)

Coupled with the claims of Christ, the promises of God, the testimony of the Holy Spirit, and the New Testament affirmation and application of the gospel, we can summarize Biblical Faith as the simple, certain persuasion that:

- Jesus is Real ("He exists" - Hebrews 11:6);
- Jesus is Right ("Assurance of things hoped for and conviction of things not seen" - Hebrews 11:1); &
- Jesus is Better ("He rewards those who earnestly seek Him" - Hebrews 11:6).

First, we must believe Jesus is real. We may find helpful lessons from fables, but what we will never find is true salvation.
As Paul put it in 1 Corinthians 15:17, "If Christ has not been raised, then your faith is futile and you are still in your sins."

Second, we must believe Jesus is right. Christ is all or He is nothing, and genuine faith requires that we surrender fully to His will, wisdom, word, and ways. While He openly invites all, Jesus is clear that we can only truly come if we are willing to deny ourselves, take up our cross, and follow Him (Mark 8:34).

Finally, we must believe Jesus is better. Genuine faith takes Jesus at His word and embraces Him:
- As the bread of life who alone can satisfy our hungry souls (John 6:35);
- As the light of the world who shows us the truth of who God is and who we are (John 8:12);
- As the door who gives us access to the Father (John 10:7);
- As the resurrection and the life who gives us a sure hope that not even death can steal from us (John 11:25);
- As the good shepherd who leads us in the paths of righteousness for His name's sake, provides for us, and protects us from every enemy (John 10:11; Psalm 23);
- As the way, the truth, and the life who leads us into the fullness of who God is and all that He has for us (John 14:6); &

- As the true vine who alone can give us full and fruitful life, not only now but for eternity (John 15:1).

What Faith Does

As we have seen from the beginning, knowing Jesus, loving Jesus, and following Jesus are all essential elements to a life of true faith. This is equally true whether someone is 8 years old or 80 years old, and whether they're starting from a place of "Pre-Gospel," "Pro-Gospel," or "Anti-Gospel." Yes, it may look different or be expressed in different words, but all of these must be present in those who believe Jesus is right, real, and better than anything else the world has to offer. In other words: knowing, loving, and following Jesus is what faith does, and where any of these are absent, there is no faith.

Faith Knows Jesus

The first evidence of genuine, Biblical faith is knowing Jesus truly. As disciple-makers, we have the opportunity and responsibility to help others:

- Articulate the gospel in a simple, clear way;
- Understand the significance of the cross;
- Identify themselves as sinners in need of grace; &

- Affirm that God loves them because of His mercy and not because of any good works that they have done or will do.

Faith Loves Jesus

The second evidence of genuine, Biblical faith is loving Jesus deeply. As disciple-makers, we have the opportunity and responsibility to help others:
- Develop personal rhythms of Bible reading, prayer, and worship;
- Ask questions about God's word and how it applies to their lives;
- Believe God's promises; &
- Grow in love for God's people (the church).

Faith Follows Jesus

The third evidence of genuine, Biblical faith is following Jesus faithfully. As disciple-makers, we have the opportunity and responsibility to help others:
- Obey Jesus *because* they're loved, not *so that* they will be;
- Repent for sin when they see it; &
- Show the fruit of the Spirit more and more in their lives.

"The fruit of the Spirit is love, joy, peace, patience, kindness, goodness, gentleness, faithfulness, and self-control." (Galatians 5:22-23)

The church will never make the impact on the world that Jesus commands us to until:

1. We understand what we believe and why we believe it;
2. We speak humbly and boldly about our beliefs;
3. We live consistently with what we believe; &
4. We love those with whom we disagree.

This is a true gospel counter-culture. This is what genuine faith looks like. This is what Jesus calls us to, and we have the responsibility and the privilege of inviting others to join us as we grow to know, love, and follow Jesus together by His grace.

ANTI-GOSPEL SUMMARY

ANTI-GOSPEL

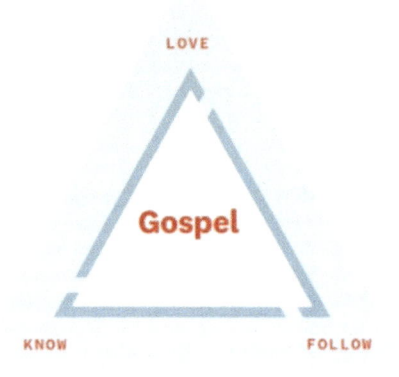

LOVE

Gospel

KNOW FOLLOW

PRE-GOSPEL PRO-GOSPEL

DESCRIPTION

- Inaccurate knowledge of the gospel, negative view of the Church/Christianity.
- Has heard the truth of Jesus and rejected it. There is a dismissal of (if not distaste for) the gospel because of various negative personal experiences, ranging from poor treatment by Christians to negative cultural depictions of Christianity to lack of belief in the truths taught in Scripture. Often people in this category are not rejecting Jesus as much as they are rejecting a caricature of Jesus.
- This is the dominant cultural view in America.

NEED

- The core need of those in this posture of unbelief is to LOVE Jesus.
- Titus 2:10 calls us to live our lives "so that in everything [we] may adorn the doctrine of God our Savior."
- As Christians, we have the privilege and the responsibility of not only sharing the truth of Jesus, but also living the gospel out in front of those who don't yet believe, trusting that God will use our faithfulness to adorn His gospel before a watching world.

DISCUSS

1. Where have you encountered this Anti-Gospel posture of unbelief (in yourself or others)?

2. Is there anyone in your life right now that you've written off? How do the grace and truth of Jesus correct this perspective?

3. In your opinion, how has the Church earned a bad reputation in the culture? What should a healthy Gospel Counter-Culture look like?

4. When you face opposition to what you believe, do you tend to retreat into silence, pick a fight in pride, or engage in humble confidence?

5. Where have you been fooled by counterfeit faith? Why can this be so convincing?

6. Why are all 3 parts of a Biblical definition of what faith is essential (pg. 138-141)?

7. Re-read the Anti-Gospel Summary (pg. 144-145): What's new? What's confusing? What's hard? What's exciting?

Appendix 1

The Gift Of Repentance

When Martin Luther said that "Jesus Christ willed...the entire life of believers to be one of repentance," he was pleading with all who would listen to see and hate our sin as God does. More than that, he was trying to help us understand that the grace Jesus bought for us at the cross is always enough. If we define repentance as "turning our back to sin and our face to God," then the question we need to ask is: "How do I do that?" And the answer, very simply, is by the grace of Jesus.

As Christians, we would all agree with that statement, but do you really live like it's true when you're confronted with sin in your own life? When you sin, do you tend to run away from God in guilt or run to God for grace? If you tend to run away from Him in guilt, shame, or fear, then you need to ask an even deeper question: What do you believe is at stake when you sin: God's delight in you or your delight in God?

The more we understand that the love, delight, acceptance, and favor of God is based on Jesus and His work for us and not on our work for Him, the more we're set free to run to God when we sin, desperate for the grace that only He can give and confident that He has already given us all we need in Jesus.

Repentance then, at its core, is a relational act. It isn't a transaction by which we earn acceptance, salvation, or forgiveness; that's all been done already by Jesus in His death and resurrection. Rather, it's the restoration of our relationship with God that our sin has kept us from rejoicing in.

In other words, we repent because we want more of God Himself and our sin is keeping us from experiencing the joy, life, peace, and rest in Him that Jesus died to give us.

Once we begin to see this, repentance becomes a blessing instead of a burden because, as sinners, it is our surest path to true and lasting joy in our relationship with Jesus. But what should this kind of repentance look like?

Step 1 | Be Honest
(1 Corinthians 11:28; 2 Corinthians 13:5)

If we want to grow in knowing, loving, and following Jesus, we must be committed to living according to His Word.
All true repentance begins with honest, deep, Biblical self-evaluation rather than a quick check of cultural and church norms or comparing oneself to others.

Questions
- Where am I disobeying God's commands?
- Where am I not believing God's promises?
- Where am I not delighting in God's character?
- Where am I living for myself and not for Jesus?

Action Steps
- Name your sin Biblically.
- Ask what sinful motives led to your actions.

Step 2 | Be Humble
(Luke 18:9-14; James 5:16; 1 John 1:9)

If the Bible is true then sin should never catch us by surprise. Therefore we should be quick to doubt ourselves rather than scared of being "found out" as a sinner in need of grace. As this happens, we will be set free from self-protection and self-promotion, and we will be driven to confess our sins as Scripture commands because we have nothing to lose and everything to gain.

Questions
- Why am I so afraid of being sinful?
- What's keeping me from confessing my sin to God and others?
- How am I being controlled by the opinions of other people?
- Who am I trying to impress?

Action Steps
- Confess your sin to God and others.
- Acknowledge your need for both forgiveness and help.

Step 3 | Be Hopeful
(2 Corinthians 12:9, Colossians 2:13-15)

We can only be honest and humble if we know that the grace of our God will be enough to bear the full weight of our sin. Therefore we must cultivate a deep, rich understanding of this grace by remembering what God has done for us in Jesus, resting in the promises of His Word, relying on the work of His Spirit, and rejoicing in the truth that God's grace is power.

Questions
- How have I experienced the grace of God most powerfully in my life?
- Where in Scripture does God promise to be gracious to me?
- What most often takes my eyes off Jesus and turns them in on self?
- Where do I need to believe the gospel isn't just true…but it's true for me?

Action Steps
- Trust that Jesus paid for this specific sin on the cross.
- Rest in God's grace for both forgiveness and victory.

Step 4 | Be Happy
(2 Corinthians 1:20; Galatians 5:1; 2 Peter 1:3-4)

If repentance does not lead to joy then it is not true repentance. As mentioned above, repentance is the process through which we, as sinners, are restored to right relationship with our strong and beautiful God. And because our God is stronger than anything we fear and more beautiful than any temptation we face, we can live in freedom and joy only when we find that life in Him. We don't repent to get God's blessings, God's forgiveness, God's favor, God's love, or God's grace. We repent to get more of God. And when we do, He is faithful to give us all that we need.

Questions
- Why am I repenting? What do I hope to gain?
- Where am I repenting half-way and still trying to hold onto my sin?
- What's keeping me from the joy Jesus promises to all who surrender everything to Him?
- Is more joy in Jesus worth whatever it may cost? If so, what's holding me back from repentance right now?

Action Steps
- Take hold of God's promises.
- Live joyfully in the freedom of your new identity in Jesus.

Appendix 2

The Gospel

Are you looking for meaning? For joy? For love? Are you looking for justice? For beauty? For peace? Are you looking for community? For identity? For purpose?

If so, then we have good news. If you've been looking for all these things and keep coming up empty, it can be tempting to think that you'll never find them.

But what if you've been looking in the wrong place? What if they were always available to you and you simply never reached out and took hold of them?

The gospel (God's story about Jesus, the world, and you) is the good news that you've been needing to hear because it tells you where to look to find the life you've always wanted and never dared to hope was possible.

LOOK UP ↑

The gospel, like all stories, starts with God (Genesis 1:1), who created and rules over all things as a loving Father (Ephesians 3:14-21) and good King (Isaiah 37:16). God created men and women to rule with Him as beloved children (1 John 3:1) and faithful servants (1 Peter 2:16), finding true and lasting joy only in knowing, loving, and following Him.

LOOK IN ↓

From the beginning, we have believed the lie that God isn't enough for us (Genesis 3:1-7). By living for ourselves, rejecting God's love, and fighting His rule in our lives, we have all rebelled against our Creator and become His enemies (James 4:4). As a result of this rebellion, which the Bible calls sin, we all have to face the fact that we've lost the joy, love, and freedom we were made for. And if that's the whole story, we have no hope because we're all just waiting to receive the punishment of God that our sin deserves. But thankfully that's not the whole story. Something happened that changed everything.

LOOK BACK ←

When God saw that His children had rejected Him and become His enemies, He could have destroyed us…but He didn't. Instead God pursued us as He always planned (Genesis 3:15) by sending His own Son, Jesus:
- To be born as a man like us (Galatians 4:4);
- To live a life of perfect obedience to the Father for us (1 Peter 2:22);
- To die as our substitute in judgment (1 John 2:1-2);
- To rise back to life, guaranteeing victory over sin, death, and hell to all who trust Him (1 Corinthians 15:20-28); &
- To reign over all things at His Father's right hand forever (Colossians 3:1-4)

At the cross, God "made Him who knew no sin (that is, Jesus) to be sin for us so that in Him we might become the righteousness of God." (2 Corinthians 5:21) He did all this so that "whoever believes in Him should not perish but have eternal life." (John 3:16)

LOOK FORWARD ➡

Jesus is calling all of us to know, love, and follow Him together but we can only look forward in hope if we're looking back in faith. For those who have never responded in faith to this good news but desire to do so, we encourage you to use Appendix #1 | The Gift of Repentance to walk them through how to take their next step.

Made in the USA
Monee, IL
17 November 2021